OVER THE GAP

DAVE PATTERSON

Media

Over the Gap
Copyright © 2009 by David Patterson/dpa Media

For information about this title or to order other books and/or electronic media, contact
the publisher:
dpa Media
1421 E. Broad St., Suite 249, Fuquay Varina, NC 27526
www.overthegap.com
919-524-1584

Library of Congress Control Number: 2009935042

ISBN: 978-0-615-31620-8

Printed in the United States of America

Book and Cover design by: 1106 Design

Table of Contents

Acknowledgements

ORKING WITH INDIVIDUALS at the Employment Security Commission and helping groups at local gatherings land jobs using the processes in this book were extremely rewarding. Experiencing the excitement of watching people discover their true worth and landing jobs they dreamed of are experiences everyone should have. The most valuable thing I learned throughout this process is that it's all about people helping one another to overcome the challenges they face and to learn that they have within themselves the skills, courage, and knowledge to become anything they want.

This book would not have been possible without the efforts of the team of people that helped pull it all together: Charles Crawford, Carrie Cantor, Sharon Garner, Elaine Lanmon, Robin Quinn, Graham Van Dixhorn, Susan Kendrick, and Michele DeFilippo and her team. Many thanks for the patience and effort you all put into making this book a success.

To all those who encouraged and supported me through the entire process, my immediate and extended family and friends, thank you, you're the best.

And especially to Helen, whose conversation and coaching led me to follow my passion and take the road less traveled, thank you.

To Micki, who gave me the positive support, patience and encouragement through the long hours and late nights that made this book a reality: I thank you with all my heart.

Dedication

To those who have the courage to take control of their destiny and future, this book is for you.

Introduction

"Chance favors the prepared mind."
— Louis Pasteur

Millions of people today have been displaced by cutbacks and downsizing. Since you've picked up this book, you may have been impacted by the economic downturn and may be one of the displaced employees that companies have let go in order to save their businesses. Due to the impact of the recession, both in the U.S. and globally, unemployment has skyrocketed, creating a hypercompetitive and unpredictable job market for people looking for employment and for professionals in transition. This highly competitive job market has left many people wondering how to compete and secure a position that will carry them through these unpredictable times.

Approaching the job market today the same way it was done a few years ago will no longer land the job or career you want. You must have a job-specific résumé, cover letter and branded value proposition integrated in all communications for each job and position. This will increase your chances of scheduling an interview and decrease your chances of having your résumé land in the "toss out" stack.

This book will help you identify your strengths, find the best career fit, brand yourself, actively promote your brand, network, interview, develop target marketing strategies and résumés, plus a method for articulating a clear value when speaking to the executives who do the hiring. It includes the best of what the Internet has to offer in dealing with today's job market, combined with how to effectively apply talents and form successful strategies to land the job you want or to transition into a new career.

The links and resources in this book will:

- Help build a foundation centered on understanding who you are.
- Help determine your unique selling proposition.
- Give you the keys to developing your branded value proposition.
- Help with research, developing target markets and networking strategies.
- Give you interactive forms and solutions to raise your profile, promote yourself and articulate your value.
- Provide a resource and templates for direct-mail campaigns, setting goals, tracking your successes and more.

In conjunction with the exercises and success strategies in this book, its purchase gives you the opportunity for up to two free coaching consultations and an additional discounted coaching session *(60% discount)* with an experienced certified career coach. This will help you maximize your potential and jumpstart your efforts.

Why is coaching being offered? Because it is a highly valuable, personalized method that top performers, executives, and people in transition use to create success, shift their thinking into a new perspective, and achieve goals that deliver the results they want in their lives. Whether your goal is to land a new job, transition into a new career, or explore different strategies and ultimately achieve success in your life, a coach will help you reach your objectives faster and with greater clarity.

To register for your coaching session, find additional interactive forms and receive a free assessment, valued at more than $200, go to: *www.overthegap.com.*

Forms Used In This Book

The Appendix contains examples of forms and templates designed to be used in conjunction with the processes mapped out in this book. These forms can be downloaded at *www.overthegap.com*.

CHAPTER 1

CEO of Me Inc.

*"The golden opportunity you are seeking is in yourself.
It is not in your environment; it is not in luck or chance,
or the help of others; it is in yourself alone."*
— ORISON SWETT MARDEN

NO MATTER FOR WHOM YOU WORKED or what your title was, start thinking of yourself as the Chief Executive Officer (CEO) of your own company–Me Incorporated. It's important to understand that you're actually a product, a product comprised of the years of training and skills developed or acquired that have proven valuable to past employers and offer value to potential employers who are looking for those specific skills and talents.

Companies interested in hiring must consider you a valuable addition, an essential component that makes them more efficient and competitive and contributes to their overall growth. Surviving in a hypercompetitive job market and setting yourself apart from competitors requires differentiating, reinventing and rebranding yourself as a product. Just as companies look for ways to maintain their competitive edge by constantly reinventing and repackaging their offerings to be more appealing and competitive, as a valued component and the CEO of Me Inc., looking for ways to improve the value of your product (you) is key to your success.

Keys to Success

It is common for advertised positions to receive responses from up to a thousand people; so companies can be selective in hiring candidates who deliver essential skills, traits, or a needed component that adds value. The following factors are critical and key to having success in securing your next job or career:

- Be innovative—Show how you used skills, personality, and knowledge to tackle challenges, and how you created solutions that impacted efficiencies, profits, and competitive value.
- Communicate clearly—Deliver a strong yet concise message about the value and benefits of your skills with an example of that value and the impact it made in similar situations and challenges that the company or executives are facing. Additionally, employers need people who can articulate a company's position, direction and or value to others within the company and with customers or clients.
- Execute a plan—Companies have deadlines and goals; they need people with the capacity to deliver and meet their expectations. When managing your time and effort, utilize procedures and processes in this book to develop skills for setting goals, staying on target and developing a methodology for organization and execution.

Strategic job hunting requires understanding who you are and the best fit for your personality. Consider top options for career selection and industry sectors within specific markets where you can enjoy success. Brand yourself and communicate that brand value in all of your communications — especially your elevator speech and value proposition, along with your résumé, business cards, e-mails, and interview techniques. Research, research, research. Spend time researching the companies you want to work for so you understand their culture, latest business trends, management, and products. And finally, get out and network with as many people as possible. Find out if your contacts and networks can help solve the challenges of some of the other people you've met. Be authentic–people connect with those they trust.

Whether applying for a position in your current industry or starting a career in a different industry, it is important to communicate skills and personal assets in a concise, well-thought-out manner that ties a value to an employer's needs relative to the skills listed in your cover letter, résumé and conversation. An integrated and clearly articulated branded value proposition in your communications will convince a prospective employer that your skills are applicable to the particular position you are applying for, even if it is not the same as a previous position, or even the same industry you worked in before. Additionally, a strong branded value proposition will command a higher price in salary negotiations.

If you want to become a sought-after professional, use the processes in this book along with the interactive tools to create strategies and tactics that will help you achieve competitive domination. The process combines best practices with interactive tools and proven methodologies to prevent one from being seen as a cog in some machine, to being perceived of as a valued component combining job titles, degrees, certifications, and achievements that can be used across multiple industries with the skills recruiters and employers look for.

Managing Your Time

Plan your day like a CEO or president of a company; develop a systematic approach to time management. Whether you're currently employed and looking to change jobs or careers, or unemployed and seeking employment, divide your time into two categories:

> **Pay Time**–These activities have the potential to bring in revenue or meet the goals that are tied to revenue opportunities, such as your job search.

> **Non-pay Time**–These are activities that don't bring in revenue but are important for other reasons. This includes time for administrative activities, meetings, lunches, research, exercising, and activities to lower your stress.

Maintaining a balanced effort during the week to include activities for your health and mental attitude is very important and should be a priority. As with any business, if the company is not balanced or too much effort is placed in one or two areas, the company will eventually suffer and be at risk of failure. Putting too much effort into only one activity and neglecting others that keep your mental attitude strong will eventually have an impact on how successful you are.

On Sunday night, begin your week by getting organized for Monday. This simple step eliminates stress and energizes you. Schedule events for the week ahead, go through last week's notes, and target a list of people to contact again. To set the tone and momentum for the following week, set appointments for Monday, Thursday or Friday. Keep a portion of Friday open for calls.

At the end of the day, do your best to focus on positive activities; this will help you feel better about your efforts and the objectives you establish for the next day.

Schedule follow-up calls for early or late in the day. The best time to reach contacts is when they're not in meetings, generally 7:30 to 9:00 a.m., lunchtime, or after 5:30 p.m. Tuesdays are one of the best days to call, as is Friday (except Friday afternoon in the summer). In the summer, Monday morning before 10:00 a.m. is good, as people are settling in after the weekend. Making cold calls on Mondays during the winter is less productive.

Think Outside The Box

Flexibility is important in today's challenging market. Learn to think outside the box. Psychologists, coaches, and doctors will tell you that most people restrict their opportunities and successes because of limitations they create or place on themselves. If you want to be a serious candidate for a better position or greater opportunity, don't put any limits on your thinking; be careful not to place limitations in terms of new opportunities for employment and growth. Think like a company competing for market share. What do you need to change to be more competitive? How will you get there? Who can help you?

Just because a job has a specific list of requirements, a 100% job fit is not always required, regardless of what is advertised or stated. Sending a letter to the senior executive, directing attention to strengths and a successful background that indicates experience in solving challenges at the level the executive is looking to fill is a great strategy.

Take a multipronged approach when seeking the best job opportunity with the greatest emphasis on networking. Don't spend days and time responding to jobs on the Internet and think it's being productive. To maximize efforts and land the best job, invest time in the following channels:

- Networking provides a 70% to 85% return on landing a job.
- Working with recruiters generates a 7% to 10% return.
- Responding to jobs on the Internet delivers a 2% to 3% return, at best.
- Using a mail or fax service to "blast" a résumé and cover letter is less than 1% effective.
- Direct mail, in combination with information gained from networking, has a relatively high probability, in the 30% success range.

Taking Care of Your Mental Health

Optimism is essential. Remind yourself that even though the market is highly competitive, opportunities exist and doors will open for individuals who establish themselves as professionals with solutions for prospective clients and employers. Your mental attitude and view of the employment market are as important to your success as how you approach opportunities.

You can increase chances for employment by using several of the techniques world-class athletes and winners use to focus on their goals and successes: use vision creation techniques and success principles in combination with a program for better health and exercise. These techniques, which visualize your having reached your goal while creating the mental feeling and sensation of what it feels like to have reached the goal, have been used for decades. There are software applications such as Orange Peel that enable people to create vision boards on their computers, and then spend time during a portion of each day visualizing their successes with visual aids. Writing out daily and monthly successes on forms like the ones in the Appendix that can be downloaded will help the mind connect with positive emotions, and when combined with visualization exercises creates a winning combination.

Searching for a job or transitioning to a new position is one of our culture's highest stress-producers. Keeping mentally and physically fit is essential, but that's easier said than done. Consider putting a process in place to ensure that you can manage the stress you will face. One of the best ways is to maintain a healthy diet and engage in regular exercise. Also, be sure to take time out from the job search to engage in pleasurable activities such as hiking, listening to music, and playing with your children or pets, all of which help to reduce stress.

If you are a senior manager, an executive, or a director who has been in a position with a company and has recently been laid off, had your job eliminated, were downsized, outplaced, right-sized, terminated, discharged, performance-managed, fired, or transitioned-out, then you may have feelings of anger, depression, anxiety, relief, sadness, or fear. It is important that you acknowledge your feelings and give yourself the room and resources to heal. If you can't pull yourself out of a slump, seek professional help. Recognize such a step as a tool that will get you back on track.

If you've been downsized out of a job, this might be the perfect opportunity to think about whether the industry you were in or the position you had was really the right fit for you.

CHAPTER 2

Finding the Right Fit

*"When one door closes, another opens; but we often look
so long and so regretfully upon the closed door that we
do not see the one which has opened for us."*
— ALEXANDER GRAHAM BELL

WHETHER INVESTIGATING A CAREER CHANGE, transitioning in
an outplacement program, or engaging in career planning,
there is a recommended process to follow that will ensure success in
landing the job you want.

The process involves taking time to assess what other industries
your skills and personality are suited for, and to examine other opportunities in those industries or market segments. You may discover that
you would be happier and more successful in another position, or even
another industry altogether.

Without a solid understanding of who you are and to what career path
your personality traits are oriented, you will spend a lifetime dissatisfied,
unchallenged, and not as successful as you could be. Therefore, your first
step, before you answer your first advertisement or put out the word to your
friends that you're seeking a position, is to take some time to look at yourself
and identify your skills, personality traits, values, and goals so you can decide
which industries and types of positions would be most suitable for you.

Take a close look at yourself and the industry in which you're currently working. You will inevitably find that, compared to a decade ago,
you have changed, your career field has evolved, and your industry has
changed. With the traditional employment model changing to a more
contract-oriented model, you must be prepared to market yourself with

sufficient skill so that you differentiate yourself from the competition, your peers, and are attractive to employers in many industries.

People who see themselves as specialists or associated with one industry, may believe they're "locked" in to only one type of business. Others may feel that they have few available options because they're generalists with a broad range of experience. The reality is that executives and management staff of all ages are moving into new careers. Many professionals find that such choices allow them to have greater income, flexibility, and more challenges. With companies losing many of their staff members due to retirement or transitioning to a new industry, securing a job in a different industry and making a career shift is easier than it used to be. Historically, people have overrated the challenges they face and underrated their ability to contribute in areas that meet a company's objectives in a relatively short timeframe.

Understanding your personality and skill sets, along with the types of industries in which you will excel, is extremely important and will keep you from wasting your time in a career that conflicts with your personality, chemistry, and who you are. A good way to start is by taking tests that will help you assess your personality and skills so you can find the best fit. These tests or tools are called psychometric tests. Psychometric is defined as "a measurement or assessment of individual differences in abilities, aptitudes, attitudes, behavior, intelligence, and other attributes through psychological tests."

◆ Case in Point ◆

Meg, a journalist, worked for a leading New York paper and discovered that while she had the writing and editing skills to succeed, she didn't have the schmoozing skills that were a large part of getting the daily scoops and insider information. Had Meg taken some of the basic assessment tests, she would have discovered a change was needed. After years of struggling and questioning her talent, she decided to explore her desire to become an independent writer and entrepreneur. After spending months agonizing over the fear of being on her own, with its uncertainty, the risk, and wondering if she had the ability to succeed, she got into book editing. If Meg had taken the time to invest in a simple psychometric test such as the Myers-Briggs, she would have discovered that being an entrepreneur and an independent editor was better suited to her personality.

Many, if not most, of the available psychometric tools use a series of questions that have been refined over many decades to identify various types of personality traits. The results are used to align one's specific personality with various job types and careers in which one can excel.

One useful tool is the MAPP assessment, which can be found on my Website at *www.overthegap.com*. The MAPP assessment is a wonderful tool providing an analysis of jobs, how well one fits, and a list of positions and careers where you can be successful. The assessment takes approximately 30 to 35 minutes to complete.

To further your understanding of your personality, I strongly recommend taking the Myers-Briggs or the DiSC. The Myers-Briggs or MBTI assessment is the industry standard for personality traits, especially when taken in combination with the DiSC assessment or the Holland Code, available at *www.self-directed-search.com*. These will give you a well-rounded understanding of yourself and an identification of the types of industries, positions, and working environments that would be best suited to you.

Completing the MAPP, MBTI, and/or DiSC assessments, along with the Self-Branding Exercise offered in Chapter 3, will enable you to become very clear about the type of position you're looking for and give you the tools you need to clearly communicate your value proposition and the career path or job opportunity you seek.

If you don't take the time to perform a self-assessment, which enables you to define exactly the positive impact your skills, abilities, values, and work style will have on an organization, you will struggle in your marketing efforts. Taking a trial-and-error approach will lengthen your search. With the wrong approach in your job search, you could end up marketing yourself to opportunities that are probably wrong for you—and possibly sabotaging your career. The result could be self-doubt, decreased confidence, and a dead-end job with no personal satisfaction.

Once you're clear on the type of job and career you want, you will want to position yourself as the best person for solving problems, building successful teams, driving growth, impacting efficiencies, and knowing how to capitalize on an opportunity or challenge.

Take several assessments to identify and connect your skills with your personality in order to identify and target specific industries, markets, and companies. Working at a job that consumes a large part of your life and that doesn't give you any pleasure is not a good investment of your time or effort. It's much easier to enjoy your career and life by taking the time to understand where you fit. You will find that when your skills, personality, and job opportunity align, it will show in the interview process and in the offers you receive.

CHAPTER 3

Branding Yourself

"If you're not appearing, you're disappearing."
— ART BLAKEY

M ANY TYPES OF ASSESSMENTS PROVIDE A breakdown of companies, positions, industries, and market segments where you will have a greater chance for success and where your personality will best fit. Other than defining your target markets and industries, it is important to focus your efforts on assessments to create the foundation for building your brand.

You may think that degrees, titles, and other credentials speak for themselves. But such things alone, no matter how impressive on paper, will not motivate an employer to hire you. A strong personal brand enables you to stand out in a sea of competitors. It is your unique promise of value and value proposition. Your personal brand, combined with a branded-value proposition, is the most important differentiator you have to increase your opportunities in any economic climate.

So, how do you define your personal brand? A personal brand is a clear, concise, and compelling statement of the intangible benefits of your service, with a focus on nonmeasurable elements such as your passion, leadership style, culture, and work style. Your personal brand along with a value proposition that is measurable, and combines money or an element that the company you are targeting is in need of, such as driving profits, efficiencies and improving operations, in conjunction with your chemistry, gets you in the door and on the short list of candidates.

Whether you know it or not, you already have a personal brand: the fifteen words or less that your colleagues, coworkers and people you've met use to identify you. To develop your personal brand, ask yourself: What is the value equation I offer to my targeted organizations? What services or assets do I have that make me different? How do I differentiate myself from other candidates?

Use the exercises in the following self-branding section to help you think about how you would describe yourself in fifteen words or less.

You as a Product

Start imagining yourself as a product—that solves a client's (employer's) problem, delivers a benefit to your client, produces the outcome the client wants, or adds value that is missing in other comparable products (candidates). Review your strengths, skills, and the unmet needs or unexploited possibilities in a market you know well. Where do they intersect? That's where you can deliver value, differentiate yourself, and market yourself as a value-added asset to a company or organization. Make sure your product (you) and brand reflect what you desire, aligns with your abilities, fits your profile, temperament, and exemplifies your skills and assets.

It's important that you learn to communicate the scope of your knowledge and potential with a value proposition tied to your brand in all your communications, i.e. résumés, cover letters, conversations, and networking.

When going through the exercises in this book, don't overlook your ability to be flexible and versatile when meeting company challenges and applying for positions. Tie past accomplishments to the different opportunities you'd find with a new position; almost everyone can work in a broader or narrower scope. For example, sales executives generally know quite a lot about marketing, purchasing, and distribution. Manufacturing professionals are knowledgeable about administration, logistics, the control function, and the general management of businesses. Controllers will have an understanding of every aspect of a business.

Many of the "skill sets" listed below are areas of achievement recruiters and employers look for that are needed in their organizations, regardless of industry experience. These are achievements that employers, recruiters, and venture firms consistently seek in candidates. Look these over and think about which of them might apply to you, then use them in the subsequent exercise.

Acquired operations	Managed rapid growth
Administrative responsibilities	Merger and acquisition negotiator
Been a corporate officer	Multi-market experience
Been a division officer	Multi-project coordinator
Been in top management	Multi-site operation experience
Budget manager on large projects	Negotiated major deals
Built self-sustaining teams	Officer and board member
Built strategic alliances	Opened new plants
Chaired civic organizations	P & L responsibility
Chaired multifunctional teams	Procured major funds/grants
Cost-control experience	Published author of articles
Designed efficient systems	Published author of book(s)
Directed start-up	Reengineered processes
Formulated action plans	Reorganized and revitalized
Improved productivity	Served on civic boards
Improved sales/profits	Served on corporate boards
Increased positive attitudes	Served on nonprofit boards
Increased revenues	Started prototype operations
Initiated sweeping changes	Strategic planning experience
Joint ventures experience	Substantial life experience
Key committees member	Substantial staff experience
Managed complex operations	Turned around operations
Managed large numbers of people	Worked closely with top management

Self-Branding Exercise

The Self-Branding Exercise will take several hours over a few days, but is well worth the effort. It is designed to get results. The exercise offers some self-discovery and insight around what you may really want to do. You may be surprised to discover just how good you really are!

For the best results, be thorough, and, above all, be honest with yourself. Get help from your spouse or close friends. Combine the results with the assessment tools you used. The combination will enable you to differentiate yourself in a crowded job market and reduce the time it takes to find the right position.

Step 1: Make a list of every personal and professional achievement you can think of, large or small. Don't describe, just list. Use your résumé as a guide. As a memory-jogger, imagine yourself back in those situations. Don't forget about school, church, and civic activities. Most mid-career people will come up with a list of twenty-five to forty items.

Step 2: Pick out the top six to ten achievements—those that are *most meaningful to you*. Transfer them to another sheet of paper and, *for each one*, write down the following three thoughts. Answer with one or two sentences each.

- Describe the situation or challenge you faced.
- Describe your role and what you did—your actions or contributions.
- Describe the results accomplished. Quantify whenever possible.

Step 3: Using the achievement list from step one, list every activity, skill, or attribute you applied to that situation (e.g., leadership, innovative thinking, problem solving, presentations, team building, project management, organization, analysis, selling, attention to detail, and travel). Leadership and problem solving are particularly valuable skills for any position, but particularly at higher levels, so be especially alert for examples of situations in which you displayed these qualities.

Creating these lists may become tedious, but it's an important exercise. Let items repeat themselves. You want to see what patterns develop. Be thorough.

Step 4: Note the skills and activities that appear most often (the top third or so) and transfer those to another list. *Rate* (not rank) *each one* on a scale of how much you *enjoy* the activity. Use a scale of 1 to 5 or high/medium/low. Be honest. You may be really good at something you don't like.

Step 5: Note the skills and activities that rated highest in enjoyment—there are probably three or four. These are your true strengths. We all have things that we're good at. These are the items showing up most often on the list of activities. We also have things we like to do. Strengths are the things that we're good at and enjoy doing.

Step 6: Map each of these strengths to the expanded accomplishments from Step 2.

Congratulations. You now have several useful things:

- A concise, well-thought-out list of your true strengths.
- Linkage of those strengths to key accomplishments.
- Short vignettes describing how you applied those strengths to achieve results.

◆ Case in Point ◆

Leadership

With the gap created in company leadership by people retiring and the Boomer generation leaving the ranks of the employed, companies are scrambling to identify and bring in new leaders. If you're a senior leader who was displaced, many companies are hiring Boomers on a contract basis in order to train individuals they have identified as having specific leadership traits. As companies shift and change to meet an expanding and ever-changing market and economy, it is thought that the orientation toward contracting management will become the new standard.

If you find that one of your outstanding qualities is leadership, you should do what you can to communicate this fact. Your résumé and conversations need to focus on areas where you have exhibited leadership traits that have made a positive impact.

CHAPTER 4

Crafting a Message
That Sells Your Brand

"We must brand, package, and market ourselves so that we are desirable."
— FUNKY BUSINESS

HOW EFFECTIVELY YOU COMMUNICATE your achievements in short but compelling stories, and how strongly they come across in all of your communications relative to your prospective client's or employer's needs, will determine whether you're successful in differentiating yourself from other job seekers.

People are hired because of the traits, skills, and abilities that certain key descriptive phrases imply. When communicating your value and attributes, it's important to select phrases that set you apart. You need to be prepared to communicate your full range of core attributes. With more interviews being conducted via phone or virtually, the perception of qualities and how they are communicated and presented can tilt things either in your favor or against you. Carefully chosen words and phrases should be at the heart of your communication strategy. It is critical to set the stage on which to build your appeal beyond your basic credentials.

Consistency throughout your messaging is a must and is key to your success and marketability. If the message you communicate is inconsistent, then your opportunity for competing and being selected will be negatively impacted.

When there is more than one strong candidate, hiring decisions almost always come down to personal qualities—the kind listed on the following page and others that are generally mentioned during the pre-interview and in the job description. It's important that you select or find the common theme in the attributes listed by the employer and, where possible, confirmed through your network. For example, if the company is in a growth stage, they will be looking for ambitious, confident leaders who are self-starters, versatile, and team players. You want to make sure you communicate those attributes in your résumé, cover letter, and value statement, and give supporting examples as to how you've successfully used those attributes in the past.

Descriptive Words and Phrases

Think about which phrases others might apply to you and ask people with whom you have worked how they would describe you.

It's critical that you practice and formulate well-thought-out position statements; use phrases that focus on the strengths and attributes that fit the position requirements and guide your audience. This type of strategy enables you to control the conversation, at least to some degree, and to align the interviewer's questions with your answers and position yourself favorably for the job.

Now that you have identified your value proposition or brand and have selected key phrases, it's time to start crafting the different components of your communications. These components include your résumé, cover letters, elevator speech, and a two-minute drill that ties in the vignettes created in the self-branding exercise to a story format about yourself and your value proposition. You may even want to include a favorite sport you play, a talent, or the college you attended to make it more personable and to relate to your audience.

Ambitious	Organized
Analytical	Outgoing
Assertive	Overachiever
Attractive	People skills
Competitive	Perfectionist
Confident	Persistent
Creative	Personal presence/charisma
Decisive	Persuasive
Dependable/loyal	Positive/upbeat
Entrepreneurial	Quick thinker
Executive image	Recognizes talent/good recruiter
Flair for putting on events	Resourceful
Good administrator	Respected/esteemed
Good communicator	Risk taker
Good listener	Sense of humor
Good-natured/personable	Self-starter
Good negotiator	Sophisticated/cultured
Good trainer	Tactician/strategic thinker
Great motivator	Team player
Hands-on	Thinks conceptually
Innovative	Thinks outside the box
Instinct for what sells	Troubleshooter
Long-range planner	Versatile
Natural leader	Visionary

Your Elevator Speech and Branded-Value Proposition

Everything that we pay attention to in today's society has grabbed our interest in some way. The messages we're exposed to every day are enthusiastic, action-packed, and promise to deliver a value. Many of them are delivered in 30 to 60 seconds or in 10 second sound bytes. Consider the messages you're bombarded with each day on the radio, television, and Internet. Many are not only less than 60 seconds long, but also offer a visual association that's strong and creates a call to action. The messages that don't offer a visual impact give enough detail to evoke or create a call for action that makes you want to find out more.

The elevator speech and two-minute drill are your audio advertisement and answer the question: "Tell me about yourself." You should immediately know exactly what to say, without sounding overly rehearsed and stiff. Being comfortable with your elevator speech comes from practice and introducing yourself at network meetings and other business gatherings.

The elevator speech got its name because it is what you might say to someone you meet in an elevator and must impress before he or she gets off and is gone forever. From a pure selling perspective, we give sales people only a few seconds to tell us what they have that delivers a value or benefit. What we hear in those few seconds makes us want to know more because the delivery is credible, the person is authentic, and it has value, if not to us, then maybe to someone we might know or meet.

An elevator speech is your introduction. Let's say you meet an old high school acquaintance who you haven't seen in many years and just happens to be a senior vice president at a company you'd love to work for. Imagine you have only a minute or two to tell him whom you've become and why you'd be a great fit for his company.

You must deliver a branded-value proposition in your elevator speech in order to separate yourself from the other candidates. People looking to fill positions or those who create positions want someone to fix a problem or meet a challenge. To get a sense of how an employer hires people, consider how you would find, hire, and feel comfortable about hiring someone to fix your plumbing or perform an emergency repair. People looking to fill positions use the same principles we all use when we make purchases. Hiring a professional for a middle management or executive management position costs a company not only the salary, but also an additional 37% to 40% or more in training or other expenses on top of the salary. Because of the high expense over and above a person's salary, companies want to make the right decisions. Now take the thought about how you would make a decision and put it in a decision framework as if this were your company, keeping in mind the cost to the company is hundreds of thousands of dollars. What criteria do you use in making a decision that could cost your company

$300,000 to $500,000? What would make you decide on one candidate versus another? How do you want to feel about your decision? If you were at a networking event or association meeting, what type of person would stand out? How would they introduce themselves?

Your elevator speech is your personal advertising message. It is up to you to make it impressive. When you're out at meetings and introducing yourself, be sure to pay close attention to the reactions people have to your elevator speech and tweak it based on the feedback you get.

The following is an example of an elevator speech and two-minute drill with a branded-value proposition:

"I use my passion for problem-solving, my charisma, solution-oriented leadership style, and experience in business development to increase profitability in companies by an average of 39%."

"I recently took one company facing a loss of revenue and layoffs to a positive revenue stream by increasing their margins from 21% to 39% by moving marketing efforts and sales to other channels, while developing a program that resold their products through 7,000 value-added resellers. My strategic solution improved internal efficiencies by 27% and reduced the overall cost of implementation by 45%. The success of the program was profiled in XYZ's publication and the positive press, along with the impact on efficiencies and sales, raised corporate-wide profits an additional 9% or $4,500,000."

Based on what you have just learned about yourself, the above example, and remembering the important phrases and adjectives that employers respond to, sit down and write out a two-minute speech that describes your career progression. Reference your strengths or specific achievements. Add a few personal touches and comments describing you as a person as well as an employee. Go back to the Self-Branding Exercise and the information you put together and use it to help create your elevator speech.

Read your elevator speech and two-minute drill aloud to ensure it's no longer than about two minutes. Then read it again about a dozen times to learn (but not memorize) it well. If you have a recorder, record it, practice it, get comfortable with how you deliver it, and state your branded-value proposition in relation to your elevator speech.

Do not discount your achievements and what you accomplished in the past, the skills you used, and the successes you've had and build them into your elevator speech and two-minute drill. At some point, everyone has made a significant impact that helped an employer gain some benefit.

◆ Case in Point ◆

Jakub, a technical writer, was displaced when the company he worked for was acquired by new management. During our initial discussions, all Jakub would focus on when asked what difference he made to his past employer was regarding changes to documents and the types of documents he had worked on. With a little more conversation and digging a little deeper, Jakub mentioned a change he made to a software program that helped with printing the documents. Jakub had rewritten the code and made some alterations that reduced the time it took to produce the documents and eliminated additional time on corrections and review. His effort saved the company hundreds of hours in employee time, with a positive impact on hard costs valued in thousands of dollars to the bottom line and efficiencies.

Cover Letters

Cover letters are extremely important and will open doors for you. Take your time to develop a cover letter for every job that is specific to that job. Keep the letter short, direct, and not more than three paragraphs on a single page.

Employers want individuals who have solved problems specific to their challenges, so you need to capture their attention at the very beginning. Typically, an executive will look at the first paragraph and then merely glance over the rest of the cover letter, so you must make it unique, simple, and interesting to read. Therefore, your lead statement must be direct and communicate a great deal of information about your skills and ability to solve the company's challenges and the benefits you deliver.

Following are the four steps that are key to a good cover letter:

1. **Grab attention** in the first sentence and/or heading. The opening should specify your reason for writing and your purpose. For a position, it should state the title, how and where you found the job posting, and could relate to inside knowledge of the company you found either through networking, industry research, or a directive of the board.
2. **Arouse interest.** Make sure your letter addresses a need of the CEO, a company/corporate challenge, or requirements of the position. Use the body of your letter to lead with your best selling point, value proposition, qualifications, and potential benefits. The

tone of your letter needs to be enthusiastic and passionate about delivering a value relative to the position and job requirements.

3. **Stimulate a desire for more information** by having a clear, concise statement focused on what you achieved in a previous circumstance that solved the same or similar challenge. Include a monetary benefit or impact on company growth, and value, that it is tied to your specific brand, skills, and assets.

4. **Provide a call to action.** Restate your interest and state that you will call or be in the area and would like to meet.

When using the four steps to create your cover letter, start with the end result in mind. Consider an opening statement and body of the letter that answer the following questions:

- What is your value proposition to my company and me as an executive?
- How will you impact my bottom line, help me reduce costs, improve efficiencies, and drive growth and revenue?

When you answer these questions, you will be creating what is known as a "dollarized" value proposition. The goal of a "dollarized" value proposition is that the statement you create is designed to generate interest and get you on the short list of candidates. The statement must have value relative to the company's objectives and needs. Next, address the following questions in the body of your cover letter:

- How have you accomplished results in the past and what makes you different from other candidates? Be specific; answering with information about who you are is not enough.
- What is your brand? What are you known for and how can you demonstrate your authenticity in a way that gives the executive a sense of the chemistry you may have with his/her company?

Your "dollarized" branded-value proposition—your promise of value—must be targeted, direct, and in the opening line or paragraph of your cover letter.

If you are mailing a hard copy, use monarch-sized stationery, as this will differentiate your cover letter from others. Monarch-sized stationery is not standard; it's smaller in size, and available online and at some office suppliers. Monarch-sized paper makes your résumé and cover letter stand out.

Following is an example of a cover letter:

May 20, 2010
Mr. George Parker
Turnaround Corporation
5565 Centerview Drive
Suite 201
Phoenix, AZ 27612

Dear Mr. Parker,

I am submitting the enclosed résumé for the position of Director of Marketing posted on your Website. In addition to the requirements for the position, my background in driving an average growth of 39% through strategic initiatives, which Derek Palmer, your CEO, listed as one of the company's mission critical goals in his annual report, is an area in which I excel.

Your requirements	My qualifications
Experience in strategic marketing	Developed marketing collateral, defined product functionality, and created the market analysis and go-to strategy for the sales and support team which generated $4.6 million in sales.
Ability to provide product vision	Capitalized on the synergies and strengths of clients, internal staff, and third parties, which culminated in $8.3 million in sales and the early release of a new application.
Identify new opportunities or problems and develop fresh/ creative solutions	Determined market opportunities, developed go-to strategy, and launched a value-added reseller program to break into new markets, generating additional long-term revenue of $876,000.
Strong problem-solving skills	Contributed to an enterprise-level vision strategy by negotiating offshore alliances for product development, offsetting $534,000 in internal costs.
Results-oriented mindset	Delivered compelling business cases, leveraged channels, and built strong relationships that reduced product's time to market and drove sales and revenue ahead of deadline by eight months.

I appreciate your thorough consideration and welcome the opportunity to further discuss my qualifications and learn more about Turnaround Corporation's vision for the Director of Marketing.

I can be reached during the day at 207-555-2918 or by e-mail at bbozeman@gmail.com.

Sincerely,
Bill Bozeman

The All-Important Résumé

Over the past year, with millions of people unemployed, how résumés are read and viewed by companies has changed. The job market is flooded with résumés from résumé-blasting services, blind job advertisements on the Internet, and people just sending résumés to any position in an attempt to gain employment.

As a result, many companies have gone from seeing the Internet as a viable solution for finding qualified candidates to one that is a necessary evil. Companies have begun to see the value in hiring people recommended by other staff members and close friends. The personal recommendation acts as a great job-filtering system, and provides companies with talented people who have already been identified as having the right chemistry and skills to meet the needs of the company.

So what does that mean to you as a job seeker? First, make sure your résumé is designed to target the job requirements or a challenge the company or management is facing. Make sure everything in the opening statement and following paragraph ("above the thumb") clearly states your value proposition and skills for the position, the requirements, and/or the challenges the company is facing relative to growth, efficiencies, profit, and customer retention.

What does "above the thumb" mean? When you hold the first page of your résumé in your hands, look at what's written that is above or even with your thumbs. The information at and above your thumbs is what the person reviewing your résumé will see first. If there isn't a compelling reason to read further, in the area between and below the thumbs, then your résumé is put in the pile of unqualified candidates.

In our workshops, we always get the question, "What kind of résumé should I have that will land me the job I want?" There are many ways to design and build your résumé. The basic types identified and being used today are:

Chronological

A chronological résumé starts by listing your work history, with the most recent position listed first. Your jobs are listed in reverse chronological order, starting with your current job. Employers typically prefer this type of résumé because it's easy to see what jobs you have held and when you worked at them.

Functional

A functional résumé focuses on your skills and experience rather than on your chronological work history. People who are changing careers or who have gaps in their employment history use the functional résumé most often.

Combination

A combination résumé lists your skills and experience first. Your employment history is listed next. With this type of résumé, you can highlight the skills you have that are relevant to the job being applied for, and also provide the chronological work history that employers prefer.

Targeted

A targeted résumé is one that is customized so that it specifically highlights the experience and skills relevant to the job you're applying for. It takes more work to write a targeted résumé than to just apply with your existing one. However, it's well worth the effort, especially when applying for jobs that are a perfect match for your qualifications and experience.

Mini Résumé

A mini résumé contains a brief summary of your career highlights and qualifications. It can be used for networking purposes or shared upon request from a prospective employer or reference writer who may want an overview of your accomplishments, rather than a full-length résumé.

We tell our workshop clients that they should have more than one résumé and that each one they send out must be tailored for the specific position and company to which they are applying. We strongly recommend that the résumé contain a branded-value proposition and be target specific. Additionally, I recommend that the flow and message be consistent between the cover letter and résumé.

Formats, Recruiters and Degrees

Prior to this hypercompetitive job market, there were basic standard formats and guidelines to use for résumé writing. Since the beginning of the recession, there have been many changes. Use the Internet for examples of résumés to get the most up-to-date résumé layouts.

Once you've established your résumé outline and format, you need to identify recruiters in your industry with whom you can work and network to land a job. A general rule with many recruiting firms, and from a general marketability standpoint, is the more substantial your education, the greater your marketability. In instances where you are being compared to other candidates where achievement levels, versatility, and previous employers might be equal, your education level, activities, and associations have an impact. This is especially true in larger corporations. (However, networking, personal introductions, and recommendations have been known to trump degrees.)

Having disadvantages from an educational and credentialing standpoint requires a more aggressive and finely tuned search designed to eliminate or reduce your chances of not being competitive. Credentialing and certifications from nationally recognized sources will, in most cases, offset not having a master's degree. Many companies view experience, achievements, and recent certifications as a plus because they are more current with economic and global business challenges.

Even though a specific degree will improve your opportunity to get your résumé on the right pile when working with recruiters and applying for Internet postings, you do not want to put too much weight on degrees. You'll have greater success with strategies that focus on differentiators, strengths, and successes, no matter the type of degree. Focusing on skills used and challenges where you have made specific impacts will earn you the right to be selected for an interview and an opportunity.

If you don't have particularly impressive educational credentials, or even if you do, play up such things as memberships in industry associations, industry leadership positions, copyrights or patents you hold, and medical certifications.

Volumes have been written on how to write a winning résumé. You can get good results by using a well-recognized and credible résumé-writing service. If you do elect to use a service, make sure the individuals working on your résumé are experienced and certified professional résumé writers. If they do not hold a certification, you're better off writing your own. Using a credible service is generally worth the money and will enable you to better utilize your time in productive activities, such as networking. The end product from a professional résumé writer will set you apart from the competition and will be one more differentiating factor in your favor. Image is critical, and to differentiate yourself from your competitors, do not use standard assembly-line materials for your résumé and cover letters. Get quality paper that looks professional and projects a polished, professional image.

Consider having the text on your résumé right justified with enough space in the margin for making notes and highlighting. This type of format allows you to use the left-hand margin for handwritten notes when mailing the résumé to senior executives. Adding a note lets you comment on something the senior executive's company has done or needs help with, highlighted next to a quantifiable action or result you previously achieved, on your résumé.

Guidelines for Résumé Writing

1. Be specific about the position for which you are applying. Mention the position in the opening statement in your résumé.
2. Include a compelling and strong branded-value proposition that is tied to your target's specific needs and/or management's challenge in the first two paragraphs (or in the space above your thumb if you are holding the document in your hands).
3. Image counts. Make sure your résumé is distinctive and stands out. Highlight key words or phrases that are specific to the requirements of the position. Use the best quality paper available and make sure there is consistency between your cover letter and résumé.
4. Minimize any liabilities in your résumé. Focus on your strong points in the opening statement and throughout. Don't draw attention to shortfalls in skills or length of employment.
5. Clearly communicate your skills, assets, and benefits. *Always* lead with a branded-value proposition that is key to the company, employer, management, and executive directives for the position and job requirements.
6. Make sure your résumé is in a format that works with résumé-scanning software, especially if you are applying for jobs online. Research the best format to use. Keep in mind that you will have only a 1% to 2% success factor landing a job online using the major job boards. Use company Websites for better results.
7. Your résumé needs to be flexible so you can manipulate the information and change it for multiple markets and opportunities. Your résumé is your calling card. One thing that will differentiate you

from other applicants is having a flexible format you can change to highlight specific skills and jobs relative to the employer's needs. One size doesn't fit all when it comes to résumés and jobs.

Now that you've crafted your brand and have a strong résumé, Chapter 5 will give you tips on how to promote your personal brand.

CHAPTER 5

Promoting Your Brand

"The primary focus of your brand message must be on how special you are, not how cheap you are. The goal must be to sell the distinctive quality of the brand."
— KERRY LIGHT

PROMOTING YOUR BRAND IS ESSENTIAL if you want to be continuously sought after. Think of yourself in terms of a Yellow Pages advertisement and plan how best to demonstrate your value as a product to the type of organization in which you would like to work. Launching a personal public relations (PR) campaign for your brand will help you get the word out and expand your network.

Use the following steps in your self-promotion, and you'll find that you have companies and individuals contacting you with opportunities.

1. Stay visible in your industry or market. You can do this by publishing three or four white papers per year that address an industry problem and solution. In combination with publishing white papers and articles, speaking in front of groups will build your reputation and credibility.
2. Take advantage of PR opportunities. Go online to *www.PRweb.com* and use it as a resource for generating press releases and creating your own PR. Also, *www.nakedpr.com* is a great resource for information on how to write and post press releases.
3. Promote yourself through blogs, on Twitter, Facebook, Plaxo, LinkedIn, and informative Websites.

4. Take advantage of informational interviews, i.e., meetings with anyone and everyone who might possibly be a good contact for you.
5. Write articles for industry magazines and e-zines.
6. Speak to local organizations, such as the Rotary Club or the Chamber of Commerce.
7. Volunteer in community programs to raise your profile and meet more people outside your personal circle of acquaintances. If you're targeting specific companies, go to their Websites and find out which volunteer organizations they support.
8. Publicize everything you do that's newsworthy. Be certain your press release has a solid news angle, is well written, and that you have spent time planning your distribution strategy.
9. Sign up for a targeted direct-mail campaign.
10. Network like crazy. (This is so important, Chapter 8 is devoted specifically to networking.)

White Papers and Articles

White papers and articles not only educate your target audience but also reinforce your value and position as an expert in your field. This is especially true when you combine self-marketing efforts on Twitter, Facebook, and other popular social media sites.

When writing and crafting your article or white paper, take the time to make sure you are writing about a topic or business issue useful to your reader. The downfall of most people who write white papers is that the papers do not address a relevant topic or aren't of any interest.

Some of the best and most effective tactics include writing articles in trade journals, local newspapers, and association publications. See if you can get a local magazine or online e-zine to assign you to write a profile on business leaders you want to meet. Most executives like the publicity, and small papers and magazines are always looking for articles and writers. Contact nonprofits, associations, or groups that may be looking for articles to fill their newsletters and offer to send them your articles. Write articles specific to your target market.

A great resource for writing white papers and articles is the book *Writing White Papers: How to Capture Readers and Keep Them Engaged*, by Michael Stelzner.

Social Media and Blogging

What are social media? Social media are Internet-based tools used to share and discuss information on the Internet. Individuals use tools, such as Twitter, MySpace, Facebook, and LinkedIn, to share and discuss topics of interest. In addition to these Internet sites, there are bookmarking sites like *Del.icio.us.com* and news sites like *Digg.com* that people use to organize links and save links to Web pages they want to remember or share.

If you're not blogging and using social media to promote yourself, then you're missing the best resource for marketing. Other than the general fun of engaging other people with similar interests, using social media helps with networking, establishing credibility, and collaboration. Most popular social media sites limit the length of your blog to less than 200 words. This type of microblogging enables readers to identify with the person blogging and visit their Website for more information.

Websites

If you don't have a Website, it would benefit you to establish one. Wordpress.com is free and has easy-to-install templates you can use to create your Website, with blogging capabilities and other plug-ins to make your site functional. As an alternative solution, you may want to focus on building a presence using all of the social networking sites and establishing yourself on as many of the popular sites as possible, or as many as you can keep up with. Consider establishing a site on *www.visualcv.com*. Visual CV provides online exposure and an additional presence. One word of caution—be aware of what you post, many HR departments and executives will Google your name and search popular sites to obtain information about you and to substantiate your background and history.

Public Speaking

Speaking at trade shows and at local groups such as the Rotary Club, the Chamber of Commerce, and other organizations, will impact your success and leverage your existing contacts. If you don't have experience in public speaking, consider joining a local Toastmasters club for experience, exposure, and a chance to network.

Speaking engagements can be challenging; therefore, acquire experience at small gatherings first and speak on topics about which you are knowledgeable and passionate. Combine your speaking with the topics you covered in your white papers or articles. You'll be amazed at how easy it is to speak in public and the benefit you gain as a result.

Volunteering

A great way to give back to the community is by volunteering, where you can network and learn new skills. Use the assessments you took earlier to focus on volunteer organizations where your background provides value. Research the Websites of your targeted companies, and Google the officers to find out which volunteer organizations are of interest to them or they make contributions to. Make sure you included your participation in these organizations on your résumé and as part of your social communications.

Publicize Your Events

Your involvement with an event or an announcement that you want the public to know about raises your profile and/or gains more exposure on the web or in the local community. Write an informative and appealing press release to communicate your announcement or involvement in a project and to gain exposure on the web and in your local newspaper.

If you don't have experience writing press releases, you may want to consider hiring a professional writer to put together the first one or two for you, to promote your industry knowledge and expertise. Don't discount social media; it's frequently utilized by businesses and executives to keep up with the latest trends and changes in their industry. Whatever blend and form of communication you use, make sure it's targeted at your audience. For instance, in your research, you may have noticed that the CEO of the company you want to work for was quoted in a quarterly association e-zine, community paper, or magazine. You now know your target audience reads this specific resource, so you would definitely want to print an article, white paper or press release in that resource.

Why are press releases important? In the past, they were sent to journalists to make them aware of news that might be of general interest to the readers of their particular publication. This was in the hope that they would write and publish their own article about the subject. There are mixed opinions among industry leaders today about the effectiveness of sending press releases to newspapers and magazines. The argument is that the Internet is currently used by more news agencies for gathering information than ever before. With the rise of social media and the Internet, most publications subscribe to services that scan the Internet for newsworthy press releases, blogs, articles, and white papers. However, sending press releases to local community newspapers is still practiced. If you feel you must send out press releases to the media using hard copy and mail, as an alternative strategy to attract attention, enclose your press release in a FedEx, UPS, or Postal Service Next Day Delivery envelope.

If you're going to write a press release on your own and not engage a professional writer as a resource, research the proper way to write and publish the press release, such as the "reverse pyramid," with the most newsworthy information presented first. Press releases start with a headline, an eye-catching/attention-grabbing title designed to highlight the news angle. They range from 300 to 600 words, seldom exceed a single printed page in length, and provide information that is topical enough to be of interest to journalists and bloggers. Using the reverse pyramid is a great way to blog on your Website as well as other blogging media where you're allowed space.

When constructing your press release, use the following format as an outline.

- Create a concise, yet catchy, headline.
- Write a brief summary of the news and information.
- Create and write the body of the news you want released.
- At the end of the release, provide background information about the person issuing the press release and his/her organization.
- Distribute the press release to journalists and online sites using PR Web (*www.prweb.com*) or other online services and press release distribution sites.
- Use online search engine tools and alerts to track the coverage of your PR release.

Direct Mail

You may have seen advertisements for direct mail or mail blasting, along with many testimonials and strong success claims. These services typically send out 10,000 to 20,000 pieces in their mailings.

Many executives who used direct mail services received nothing in return for the effort, or such a low return on partially qualified opportunities that it was a complete waste of their investment. The reason is that the majority of the firms offering direct-mail services send out a five- or six-line cover letter with the résumés that are simply a historical recap. The résumés are not solution or value-proposition specific and generate poor, if any, opportunities for employment.

There is some value in being in the right place at the right time and, frankly, that's what mass direct mailings gamble on while delivering a very low return.

However, a targeted and focused direct-mail campaign, with tailored letters that meet specific needs in industries where you have a strong background, profile, and history of success, can be productive, especially when strategically applied with your networking and research efforts.

When it comes to your personal marketing and PR campaign, there is no such thing as too much, as long as your focus is on sharing your knowledge and expertise. It all boils down to the intent, not the exposure. Don't take action based only on what you are going to get out of your efforts. People will notice if your efforts are being driven by your need for something other than delivering benefit and/or sharing information that has value to others, and it will erode your credibility.

As part of your self-promotion, consider taking yourself on the road and putting yourself out there by setting up lunches, breakfasts, and coffees, and going to trade shows and local meetings. Make sure your efforts are targeted to your industry and audience. Don't go to every network meeting or trade show, you'll just waste your time and effort, and your return will be marginal. Be selective—go where your target companies would go, as that is where their executives will be. When you get in front of a decision-maker, or when someone asks you what you do, make sure you're adept at delivering your 60-second commercial. Remember, you want it to sound natural, not memorized.

As part of a balanced marketing plan, never expect too much from any single channel. Always invest your time in areas where you'll have the greatest return. A well-thought-out self-marketing plan can cut your job-hunting effort by as much as 50%.

Be relentless in your pursuit of promotion opportunities. *Never* let up. Everything you do raises your profile and develops valuable relationships and opportunities that you can leverage to collaborate, build your network, and engage in future business activities.

CHAPTER 6

Doing Your Homework

"Research is creating new knowledge."
— Neil Armstrong

Knowledge Is Everything

While it is important to understand who you are and your unique value proposition, research is the underpinning and foundation for your job search. Research provides you with an understanding of the industry, challenges, key issues, and ongoing changes. You need to understand the "hot buttons" in your targeted industries, and research provides the information needed to get you there.

If you're short on information about a particular industry, the easiest way to acquire the knowledge you need is through the Internet. Using the resources available on the Internet makes it easy to develop the knowledge needed to be able to communicate your expertise and understanding of the many products, industries, challenges faced, and changes in the market. Find out who has published recent e-books and articles in e-zines and become involved in blogs and networks focused on your target industry.

With many industries today suffering from financial and economic downturns, there is no lack of opportunity to leverage your experience and create opportunities across multiple industries. The key is to make sure, based on your skills, expertise, target market, and background, that you communicate the ability to deliver the desired results. Use all the resources available to you. Being a corporation of one, or Me Inc., ask yourself how a business would accomplish this task. Where would a corporation go for information?

✦ Case in Point ✦

It had been years since Brooks had to search for a job. The sale of the company he worked for changed his future direction and he now faced the uncertainty of a poor economy, his age and only 90 days to land a job. However, Brooks had learned from his position as VP of market research at Richmond Technology Partners that research pays off.

With three month's notice from the new owners that his position was not essential, Brooks began researching local and regional companies where he knew he could provide a value. With large corporations being hit by the shift in the economy, he decided to target smaller companies.

Using online research tools such as Google and LinkedIn, Brooks got information on his target company's officers and press releases, including one article where the CEO at Jones Brothers Clinical Research stated that market research would be the future of the company and that additional funding was being allocated to grow their market research staff.

Through his network, Brooks was introduced to David Jones, the EVP of market research at Jones, and sent a letter asking him to lunch to discuss market trends.

David was so impressed with Brooks that when he returned from lunch, he called Ryan Franks, the network connection they had in common, to find out more about Brooks. The conversation was very positive.

When Brooks followed up from the lunch meeting, David suggested they get together with Ryan after work and talk shop.

Again, David was impressed with how good a fit Brooks was with the company's business model, and with his knowledge. Brooks was impressed with David's management style and vision for the future of the company, and commented on how he was able to impact the growth and market direction at Richmond Technology Partners.

Later that week, David contacted Virginia Stuart, the Director of HR, and the company created a new position at Jones. Three weeks later, Brooks accepted the new position.

Because Brooks had done his homework and knew the challenges Jones was facing, he was able to position his background, knowledge, and value in terms that demonstrated a good fit with the company and its future goals. Brooks' research and networking paid off as it landed him a solid job with a growing company where he would excel.

Resources

Many resources are available from your local Chamber of Commerce, networking organizations, and meet-up groups, such as *www.meetup.com*, where you can obtain information.

Another way to glean this knowledge is to talk with people in the industry. You can obtain information on key executives by using Google and other resources, such as LinkedIn and industry associations.

Once you've gathered information about your targeted companies or contacts, an effective tactic that has worked for many applicants is to state in your cover letter or letter of introduction, the challenge the company is facing and how you have created or developed solutions to similar challenges. This shows that you may have what it takes to resolve the company's dilemma. In addition, the information you uncover provides you with details you can use in interviews and for creating success stories based on your skills and experience in relation to a company's problems, trends, or issues.

Microsoft's Bing and Google (*www.google.com*) are probably the best resource for your research. You can search for anything and will likely get many pages to sort through. Other good sites are *www.copernic.com*, a desktop search solution, and Yahoo (*www.yahoo.com*).

Below is a short list of specific sites to use for research.

The U.S. government has resources at *www.census.gov/naics*. The North American Industry Classification System (NAICS) is the standard used by federal statistical agencies in classifying business establishments for the purpose of collecting, analyzing, and publishing statistical data related to the U.S. business economy.

NAICS was developed under the auspices of the Office of Management and Budget (OMB), and adopted in 1997 to replace the Standard Industrial Classification (SIC) system. It was jointly developed by the U.S. Economic Classification Policy Committee (ECPC), Statistics Canada, and Mexico's Instituto Nacional de Estadistica, Geografia e Informatica, to allow for a high level of comparability in business statistics among the North American countries.

For general business research on companies and individuals, use the sites listed below in combination with the sites previously mentioned.

CNN: *www.money.cnn.com*. For business news, salary comparisons, and more.

Inc.: *www.inc.com*. A great resource on entrepreneurial topics, lists the top 500 growing companies.

Business Journal: *www.bizjournals.com*. Good compilation of information and news on small businesses.

Business News: *www.topix.net*. General news topics, both nationwide and international.

World Business News for white papers: *www.conference-board.org*. Some basic information is available, but more of a membership/ pay site for information and documentation.

American Society of Association Executives: *www.asaecenter.org*. Resources are for members only. Good for networking with senior executives.

Airs: *www.airsdirectory.com*. Good information on mergers, recruitment trends, and more.

CEO Express: *www.ceoexpress.com*. Great information, plus access to other resources for research.

For venture funds information and start-ups, use *www.venturewire.com*.

Top e-zines that report on trends:

- Wired: *www.wired.com*
- Fortune: *www.fortune.com*
- Forbes: *www.forbes.com*

An easy-to-use fee-based research site is *www.1jump.com*. 1Jump is an effective way of finding out information about companies instead of using traditional search engines. With a database of more than one million company Websites, 1Jump is rated as a top business search and information engine.

And don't ignore blogs on Technorati: *www.technorati.com*. A great source for finding information on companies, as well as blogs on any topic.

For detailed information on public companies, check out:

www.bloomberg.com
www.edgar-online.com
www.sec.gov
www.vault.com

Additional websites for public companies:

www.switchboard.com
www.corporateinformation.com
www.freeedger.com
www.irion.com
www.ccbn.com
www.executivelibrary.com.

To target specific companies, and for interview information, there is no substitute for the in-depth research you can accomplish by simply visiting the websites of the companies in which you are interested. Visiting company websites combined with gathering general research on the company, owners, executives, and industry will arm you with information to tailor your cover letters and orient your résumé to fit the company requirements. Websites offer insight into business partners and the volunteer organizations they support which may prove to be an avenue of opportunity for you, especially when combined with other research resources, including information on competitors. If the company is publicly traded, obtain a copy of their 10K report, call in to the company's investors' desk for information; leave no stone unturned, as it will contribute not only to your success but will also help you make the best decision for your future.

Use the forms in the Appendix to keep notes on your target companies and develop strategies that will generate job opportunities. The forms enable you to prepare cover letters, prep for phone interviews, and network. Knowing your target companies is valuable and having access to that information at your fingertips is golden; a winning combination of knowledge and organization that will help you land the job and career of a lifetime.

You've completed the research on your target companies, now it's time to define what you're looking for within that target market.

CHAPTER 7

Defining Your Target Market

"Business has only two functions—marketing and innovation."
— MILAN KUNDERA

WHEN YOU DETERMINE A TARGET MARKET aligned with your strengths, skills, and background, you will likely find opportunities for jobs and contract employment. Many people spend their lives in high-stress jobs that they don't enjoy, simply because the work is not in line with where they will have the highest percentage of success.

Use the following questions to create a list defining your customers and target market. Validate your answers and list them against the assessments and exercises you completed earlier. If the list doesn't fit with the earlier exercises, then your success will be limited.

Consider all the resources your prospective customer uses, plus local events and activities in which they participate. Do they participate in local associations or the Chamber of Commerce? What magazines or business journals would they read? Do they contribute to any nonprofit organizations publicized on their Website?

In addition to doing research on your target market, learn to use strategic thinking and the "ripple effect" specific to hiring actions, such as a company hiring at an above-average rate and companies in high-growth mode. Consider the impact in all areas where there may be change. Make informational calls and interviews to uncover opportunities that may be created with their competitors, vendors, suppliers, and customers.

Especially in today's environment of restructuring and forced economic change, you may find a lot of reorganization and shifts in management and executive ranks. Depending on your target, consider the ripple effect down the management line to where you might find opportunity.

If you're switching industries, you'll discover that more opportunities are available in small and mid-sized (SMB) companies, as they don't have layers of management waiting to fill new opportunities. Their executives tend to be generalists and are looking for qualified talent. The SMB market is riskier and has less stability than most corporate giants. However, an entrepreneurial attitude, creativity, and being agile in one's capacity added to a solid background anchored in multiple-industry experience, are rewarded.

Much like the SMB market, venture capitalists (VCs) are constantly looking for good talent with strong backgrounds in their portfolios. VCs invest in companies to make a profit and to turn them. Most companies are in the growth stages and require people with solid backgrounds in production, operations, management, and development. In addition to being a potential opportunity, VCs can be a great networking resource. Because they are constantly looking for companies to invest in, they generally have a strong network of contacts in various industries and business sectors.

Use the forms provided in the Appendix to help identify your market. Following is an example of how one person filled out the Target Marketing Strategies form and used the questions to define and identify their target market and companies.

Identifying Target Market—Sample
In conjunction with the Target Marketing Strategies form in the Appendix, use the following example for target marketing to help develop and identify your target markets.

Who are my prospects/customers, and how will I find them?
Companies that:
- Want to improve efficiencies and business processes
- Are suffering from a loss of business
- Want to contain costs
- Are new or rebranding/launching new products or services
- Want to develop more efficient ways to grow and generate business
- Use an existing customer base and build better customer relationships
- Need sales people and business development executives

What do I provide?
- Business development
- Sales
- Marketing
- Consultant for process improvements
- Management
- Operations

What forums or media will I use to interact with potential prospects/customers? Where would my customers go and what would they read? What is, or would be, of interest to them? How would they interact with the community? How would my targeted customers find me?
- Career boards/Internet job-posting sites
- Via the Web/blogs
- Networking meetings
  - Chamber of Commerce meetings
  - Networking meet-up groups
  - Execunet-sponsored meetings (local)
  - Toastmasters
- Local Involvement
  - Volunteer groups (Jimmy V, Special Olympics—high profile groups)
  - Tennis organizations (act as organizer captain)
  - Political support groups in local government
  - Religious groups/church
- Magazine articles

Target Companies
- EMC2
- Sun Trust/banks
- RBC
- John Deere
- Eaton Corp.
- SAS
- Data Flux
- IBM

Whom do I know in these companies and how would I get an interview?
- Research LinkedIn, Twitter, Facebook, Plaxo, Google

Whom do I know who may know someone in these companies?
- Anna
- Alex
- Andrea
- Joe
- Helen for DOT (see notes for contact)
- Felix for Progress Energy contacts
- Use Chamber of Commerce as a leverage in companies listed as Chamber members
- Steve Watt

What certifications do I need, or need to be in the process of acquiring, to improve my opportunities?
- PMP, Microsoft Project

Career Sites
- CareerBuilder
- Execunet
- Netshare
- Company Websites

Recruiters
- ID industry-specific in *Red Book* (Directory of Executive Recruiters)
- Local/national/international
- Send out contact request and résumé
  - Create a hook that offers them an opportunity

CHAPTER 8

Networking for Results

"Eighty percent of success is showing up."
— WOODY ALLEN

THE UNADVERTISED WORD-OF-MOUTH job market is the largest source of new career opportunities, and the best way to access this opportunity is through networking. Networking through personal connections is, by far, the most effective way to find jobs or any kind of opportunity, for that matter. In 2001, the U.S. Department of Labor stated that less than 5% of people obtain jobs through the "open job market," consisting primarily of help wanted ads posted in print and on the Internet. In 2009, Randstad, a job placement agency, reported that close to 80% of jobs are not advertised, and 94% of those asked found their jobs through networking.

What is networking? At its very core, networking is relationship building. It's about exchanging information. And information is power for you and the people you meet. Networking creates value for both parties involved. The key to successful networking is helping others. Before you begin, you must be very clear about your value proposition and that your reason for networking is giving to or serving others, and not simply about "What's in it for me?" Helping others builds your relationships, credibility, and reputation, which then attracts people, opportunities, and business. Use networking purposefully by connecting with decision-makers or individuals affiliated with targeted employers—preferably those well positioned to make introductions and expand your connections to other hiring-decision managers.

If you haven't had experience with networking, it will take effort and commitment, and you'll have to start from scratch. Networking is not an easy thing to do if you have never done it before, but it is essential if you're going to land a position in a highly competitive job market. You'll generate the greatest success by being organized and methodical so you don't lose job opportunities for lack of persistence or action.

Before you begin, create a networking action plan and map out your goals and the outcome you desire by using the forms in the Appendix. This will help you stay focused. Be systematic. Determine to do at least one thing each day to touch your network. Tie the plan to the goals you outline in the action plan, and follow up each day with a review and posting in the daily success journal.

Determine in what activities your target contacts would engage. For example, where would they meet? To what professional or community associations would your contacts belong? Find out where they're speaking or what events they attend. If they have any audiotapes, podcasts, or are on YouTube, download, view, or buy the audio file and follow up with a letter or comment to warm them up and get their attention.

Your Online Profile

If you haven't developed an online profile, then it's time you do. Use Twitter (*www.twitter.com*), Facebook (*www.facebook.com*), LinkedIn (*www.linkedin.com*), YouTube (*www.youtube.com*), or a combination of the above, plus your Website or blog site. WordPress (*www.wordpress.org*) provides an easy way to build a blog and/or Website. Your online profile is how people see you online and it should represent you—not be just a résumé. Think of your online profile as you would a storefront in a mall. You must catch people's attention and stand out by demonstrating your knowledge and expertise. You can add value by commenting on blogs specific to your industry, on your Website, or other Websites. Use Technorati (*www.technorati.com*) to find blogs specific to your interests. Use your online presence, combined with your face-to-face meetings, to develop lists of events to attend, swap ideas, and build strong relationships by actively helping others.

Opportunities are developed through your network of advocates who understand, like, and trust you. Successful networking gives you opportunities to achieve more, expand your online presence for business through partnering, and the ability to globally build your brand. People who have a common direction and sense of communication will achieve their goals and reach their targets faster because they're leveraging and building relationships based on mutual trust.

Listing and Research

With networking, you can't succeed unless you get out, make an effort, and begin. Try out your elevator speech, your 60-second introductory speech, and put yourself out there. Determine in advance what your three best reasons or attributes are and why someone would find you of value. Make adjustments as you go, and continue to build your network.

Begin by developing a list of friends, relatives, and business acquaintances who are in industries or markets that have characteristics that fit with your background, skills, and assets. A good list will target approximately 200 individuals. If you have not networked before and are starting out, a good list would be from 50 to 100 individuals. They may be in a job or may know of someone in their network, where your value proposition delivers a true value.

Research alumni organizations and other groups you were involved in while in college or graduate school. Use the resources listed earlier to identify successful people and executives who are alums or are featured in articles, and then contact them.

❖ Case in Point ❖

Cary spent months trying to get an interview at a company he had always wanted to work for. When he finally got the interview, one of the people in the group interviewing him was a professor he had worked with more than five years ago.

As Cary sat facing the group, he wondered what impact it might have had if he'd connected and networked with the professor before now.

Once you've developed your list, prioritize your contacts as follows:

- A Contacts: Individuals with power and influence. People you know who could be of immediate influence, such as friends who work in companies and have direct contact with corporate hiring leaders, HR staff members, or senior executives who have the ability to hire directly or create positions.
- B Contacts: People you know well who may have some influence, such as neighbors and other professionals in your church or social circle.
- C Contacts: A list of people who may not know you well, but who could be helpful.

You can expand your list of contacts by using tools like LinkedIn and alumni resources. Contact your university. Get access to alumni resources or fraternal organizations. Use every available resource. Now that you have your basic list of contacts, start by reaching out to your A contacts first, B contacts second, and C contacts last.

You may also want to leverage the resources on LinkedIn to get insight and introductions to key players in small and mid-sized companies. LinkedIn is a tremendous resource for finding people in companies you've targeted and researching people on your contact list.

Networking Events

With the economic downturn, networking has become not only a way to find a job, but also a way to collaborate with other professionals and do business at all levels. Networking events are posted on the Internet on Craig's List, in meet-up forums, and LinkedIn, as well as in community newspapers, at churches, Chambers of Commerce, colleges, professional associations, and more.

When you go to a networking event, ask yourself what you want to accomplish and come away with. If you have done your homework, you'll be networking with people in your industry or those engaged in doing business in an industry or company you have targeted. Have a plan in place with an established goal. Maybe you met someone at another networking event who is looking for a video production company. One of your goals could be to find someone who can recommend a great video production company in the local area or in some other location. Your goal could be to meet three new people to add to your network. Establishing goals will help you take action and build new relationships with other business professionals. Don't be shy: shake hands, introduce yourself, and ask people what their greatest challenges have been and how they are associated with the event. Use open-ended questions to find out how you can help them or others in your network through mutual introductions. Don't hand out your business card to anyone who will accept it, use the networking event to promote your business, or for prospecting. When networking, hand your business card to contacts for whom you have a solution or those you want to connect with and brainstorm about a mutual challenge. Be genuine. Networking is about what you have to offer another person that will improve their business, opportunity, and success.

Networking is all about building new relationships. Don't waste an opportunity by making the following mistakes:

- Sitting next to people you already know
- Failing to participate in the networking part of the meeting
- Failing to read up on industry changes that you can talk about intelligently
- Engaging solely in non-conversations about sports or the weather
- Failing to plan for the event and arriving without an agenda or strategy
- Not knowing with whom you will reconnect or what you will talk about that will demonstrate your character and competence
- Forgetting to ask your new contacts how they prefer to keep in touch
- Failing to follow up with new contacts

Leave-Behinds

At small networking events, it's a good idea to have a networking profile or networking handout and a business card that has your profile, for your networking contacts to take away. The handout should provide a quick overview of your experience, targets, business sectors, and objectives, with a tag line and a short story about how you were able to make an impact.

In developing opportunities for yourself, everything boils down to the fact that you must: Have a unique value proposition tailored to the needs and requirements of the person and company to which you are marketing—one that validates your value proposition and brand (who you are and what you've accomplished), and hints of your fit or chemistry with the company you are targeting. To improve the success rate when marketing to your target channels, modify and use the sample letters in this section as templates.

Networking Handout and Leave-Behind Sample:

JEFF HOOSIER   *jeff.h@dpacoaching.com*

    D. Patterson & Associates
    1515 Cranfield Executive Center   Phone: 414-524-1587
    Washington, DC 23617   Fax: 414-524-1586

Executive coach, motivational speaker, business coach.

BA, University of North Carolina; MBA, Cambridge University; Business Coaching Certificate, Duke University.

Accomplished executive, change agent, and entrepreneurial overachiever, Jeff has grown companies an average of 39%. Jeff uses his passion for people and business, combined with leading global business initiatives, and his expertise in overcoming obstacles to launch new products, improve corporate-wide growth, and develop winning strategic business development campaigns.

- By structuring a plan to reach multiple markets, increased revenue 250% in Canadian start-up, formulating a collaborative product-development effort that created a hybrid product offering, differentiating company's products in a "me too" market to increase market share and competitive value.

- Diffused legal threats, turning around a company that went from 78 employees to 4 with no new business in three years. Developed "go-to" market strategies, delivering $8.6 million in revenue, aligned a company with a Fortune 10 corporation that resold their products across 700 resellers.

Targets:

Software	Medical	Logistics
Delta Development Corp.	Jones Clinical Research	Thompson Distribution
Richmond Technology Partners	Glaxo Smith Kline	Foodland, Inc.
EMC2	CED	

Cold Calling

Cold calling can be used to generate opportunities effectively but has a lower percentage of return without an established communication plan. An established communication plan enables you to use cold calling, not only as an introductory tool, but also for doing informational interviews and industry research. It also builds rapport in a market that you are vested in by publishing white papers, articles, and participating in speaking engagements.

Information gained from research may enable you to reach targeted executives on the phone. If you have a message relevant to their goals, you should have a good chance to get past any administrative gatekeepers.

When you're engaged in cold-call introductions and networking, make sure you have a plan to follow, with specific goals; keep your purpose straight, identify yourself, give your referral source, and explain the purpose of your call and the value that he/she will gain from the call. It's a good idea to have mentally established your goal(s) for the call, i.e., starting with the end in mind, such as a meeting date and time for an informational interview based on what you have researched. Your chances of reaching an executive on the phone will be improved if you can say that you're calling at the suggestion of a recognized contact or board member. If you reach voice mail, use it effectively by leaving your phone number, the reason for your call, and a suggested meeting time. Do your best at updating your voice mail message daily, as it delivers a professional image and provides callers with your schedule for returning calls if you are out of town.

Since many executives arrive early and leave late, schedule your initial and follow-up calls before 8:00 a.m. and after 5:30 p.m. when you're more apt to make a connection and get a good response. Make sure you have an agreement on the next steps and that there is absolute clarity about how and when you will follow up.

Instead of being reluctant to use the phone, see it as a tool to generate more opportunities and connect with people. Actually, the more you use the phone, the more confident and proficient you'll become at building relationships virtually. With 90% of all job seekers reluctant to use the phone, using it will differentiate you and help convey a sense of personal confidence and urgency. With the cost of travel in mind, many executives are using the phone more to create first impressions and to project a good image of themselves and their company. The same holds true for administrative assistants and other officers of the company.

Tips for Handling People Who Screen Your Calls

Always use the name of the person who is screening the call. In most cases, once he or she has been identified, his or her manner and attitude will become more personal.

When calling, always identify yourself and associate yourself with a company or organization. As a general rule, the more difficult and expert the screener is, the more valuable that person is likely to be, especially as an ally and resource in your future relationship with the company.

If you don't get through on the first attempt, and you can't get a good time to call back, suggest a time when you will call the screener back.

Don't leave messages until you establish direct contact with the person with whom you want to connect.

When you call back and you happen to get the receptionist or have been connected to a person taking calls, use the person's name you are trying to reach and make a statement like, "Since he (or she) is so hard to reach, would you like to do me a small favor?" If the person you're speaking with suggests that they connect you with the screener, state that you have spoken with (state the name of the screener) and you are calling back to set up a meeting, conference call, or other form of connection with the person you want to contact. Then ask, "May I call back at one o'clock or three o'clock [always offer one or two options, or ask when they would suggest is a good time to call] to see if he would be interested in speaking with me directly for a few minutes?"

The only problem with this approach is that you may be asked what the call is about. So, be prepared to leave a value statement or the name of the person who suggested you call the executive.

You can always use the call and the connection with the administrator to ask for an internal referral to another executive, decision-maker, or someone who can provide more insight and information about the company and its challenges. This request for being referred should be followed by a value and benefit statement that connecting you to the appropriate party would deliver to the company. If at all possible, do your best to develop rapport with administrators, as they have a job to do and, like everyone else, they are looking for ways to promote themselves. Always keep in mind that people who screen calls need a solid reason for providing you with information. They have to trust that you will not misuse the connection for personal gain. Coming across as being genuine and presenting yourself as delivering value and benefit will open many doors and gain you access to the right contacts.

One of the best ways to establish rapport is by mentioning recently published news favorable to the target company. You can also use the news item as a discussion topic that leads to a next step or action, to your advantage. This approach can be an excellent way to get people to help you and to set up informational interviews.

Example: "When I heard about your four quarters of growth . . . "

After a few minutes of discussion with the Administrator or Office Manager, be prepared to ask two or three penetrating questions about the organization's needs. Your research should have pinpointed several questions and topics that are executive-oriented and provide you with enough background to ask the right questions. When asked difficult questions, individuals who don't know the answer are more likely to refer you to someone who does.

If the screener asks you if you're looking for a job, be honest. Let the person know you are and paraphrase your response with a challenge the company or executive is facing and how you have solved similar challenges (your value statement) previously, and close with a request for another internal connection you could speak with if the executive is unavailable.

You may get the following comment, especially in companies that have been downsized, suffered layoffs, and undergone change: "We don't have any openings." The response: "I appreciate a person who is direct, but I have such a strong interest in the firm. With your recent growth (or a statement that is framed around a company or management challenge), I believe I could be a great asset (state your value proposition)." Close with, "Other than you, to whom can I speak that is interested in a solution to (state the company or management challenge)?"

E-mailing

E-mailing is perhaps the next best way to make contact with many people. If you're unsure how a company identifies individual e-mail addresses when using a blind e-mail broadcast (and you have identified the executive), you can use a trial-and-error method—using the generic e-mail address from the contact tab on the company Website.

One of the drawbacks to e-mails is that executives receive so many every day. Many executives at large corporations will have an assistant sift through, eliminate, and sort their e-mail. However, a well-defined and creative subject line and greeting, based on your research and targeting a company's need or an executive's challenge, will almost always get a response. Other techniques for specific jobs or opportunities have a good chance for success when they are worded properly, such as, "Executive candidate for management opportunity in business development."

If you target smaller firms, you'll always have a greater percentage of success in your e-mailing campaigns. Most small company executives will personally respond to e-mails that address one of their directives, internal needs, or potential future growth strategies. Again, make sure you have done your due diligence on the company and the executive you're contacting.

To ensure that you have a better opportunity of your e-mail reaching a top executive, make sure *there is no attachment.* Most e-mails with attachments are caught in spam filters and, if not, they are seldom opened because it takes more time than senior managers, administrators, and executives have to spend on e-mail.

Whatever method you use, make sure you have established a follow-up in some form in your communication, via either a phone call or another e-mail.

Broadcast Letters

Broadcast letters are much like e-mail blasting, fax blasting, and spamming, except in letter format. Depending on whom you ask about broadcast letters, whether a recruiter or a third party who is managing your job campaign, you will receive mixed results and mixed messages. A rule of thumb is that a 1.5% or 2% response rate is exceptional. Executives will tell you that most letters end up in the trash. Because of the cost of sending direct mail, and the time involved, broadcast letters should be used as a last resort.

Don't get broadcast letters confused with direct mail. Direct-mail programs with a focus on specific targets will deliver a greater return on your effort.

Some people have used FedEx or UPS as an effective way to get a letter to a targeted person. This strategy has worked on more than one occasion and you will have success so long as the target fits your skill set, expertise, and background, and you have a strong value proposition.

Pyramiding/Informational Interviews and Letters

If you can't immediately gain access to the high-level people you need to reach at a particular company, you should try a strategy known as informational interviewing or pyramiding. You make contact with a lower-level person and then use the name of that individual to gain an interview with someone else in the company at a higher level. With the interview approach, you're able to gain more insight into company issues, executive goals/directives, establish trust, and make additional contacts within the organization. This method also provides the opportunity for an executive to introduce you to executive management and establish an informal meeting or face-to-face introduction.

Once you feel there is an opportunity where you can deliver value and are confident that your value proposition will be of benefit based on your earlier research, review the information on *www.vault.com* for insider information on the company. This will give you an edge when meeting and discussing industry trends, challenges, and outlook.

During your conversation, ask the person you're speaking with how they feel regarding your contacting the CEO or other senior executives to explore possibilities. You may find that the person you're meeting with is open not only to suggesting a meeting but will even provide the introduction.

When asking for an introductory meeting where you need to write a short note to a senior director or executive, use something like, "In a recent meeting with Mr./Ms. X, he/she suggested that it would be of value if we were to meet. What does your schedule look like the week of _____ ?"

During your meeting, be prepared to listen 80% of the time and talk 20% of the time. Ask penetrating or open-ended questions that enable you to find out a person's or a company's challenges, and where you and your network can have a positive impact. Think of yourself as a consultant or a senior problem-solver. Learn to ask penetrating questions, listen to what the problems are, and show how you can help and deliver value. Using the Target Lead Sheet form in the Appendix, keep records of your conversations and make sure you follow up after every meeting.

When you get the opportunity to meet through pyramiding, make sure you keep the person with whom you originally met, or your contact, informed. You want the people you originally met to take an interest in your success, as it may also deliver value to them and their position. Before your meetings, make sure you've done your research on the company, the executives, particular issues, or challenges that are public knowledge, and take your notes with you for discussion. Your discussions will be brief, so make sure you have your questions prepared in advance. Your questions should be those that will segue into topics where you can tie in your value proposition and be of benefit to the challenges the company or senior executive faces.

If you're addressing CEOs and other senior executives and you haven't done your research, they will resent spending their time giving you information that you should have researched yourself. You will have greater success when you ask for feedback on specific ideas that result from your research and conversations with other executives. When asking a question of any senior executive, ask for permission. And, if you're going to ask a tough question, again ask for permission.

Consider networking with not only executives in companies you have targeted but also executives who are vendors, clients, and partners. They don't have to work at your target company to be a key connection for you and provide valuable insight and inside information.

Letter for Informational Interviewing

When using letters to establish an informational interview, use the following as a guide:

1. How you learned about the individual you're contacting, and why you're writing, i.e., what is your goal? What do you want to accomplish?
2. A brief introduction with information about yourself. Keep it brief and remember your goal is not to sell yourself but to get information.
3. Why you're specifically interested in talking with them. Show enthusiasm in expressing your curiosity about their work and their company.
4. How you can be contacted, how you will follow up, and a brief statement of appreciation for their time.

Informational Interview Sample Letter

Dear Mr. Jones: (If the person you are writing to is an acquaintance or someone you know, use Dear Bill.)

In conversations with Virginia Peterson (at XYZ company if the contact is external), we were discussing (use a topic of interest to the executive, a hot button, directive, or challenge he/she may be facing) and your name came up (or: I understand you are involved in a similar challenge or opportunity).

With my background in _____ and _____, I would like to schedule a time over lunch or coffee to hear about the solution you created and discuss what your viewpoint is on industry trends in respect to _____.

I will give you a call this _____ at _____ to set up a time to get together.

Best,

Bill Peterson

As mentioned earlier, keep the ripple effect in mind. When you see companies hiring or posting positions in one area, it could also mean that they have openings in other areas of the company. For example, if a company is hiring sales staff, it is almost a sure bet they are hiring executives in other divisions or areas.

When responding to a position for which you are highly qualified and which sounds like a perfect fit with your talents and skills, be specific in your response. Send a letter to a decision-maker. However, ensure that you have done your research on the company and the decision-makers' challenges, background, company strategies, and 10K, if they are publicly traded. Leverage your network. Ensure that your response is on target and specific to the company's needs and your value proposition. In most cases, targeting decision-makers with a value proposition directed at their needs will get you a reply. If you haven't received a reply or response within two weeks, follow up via e-mail along with a hard copy of your résumé.

Don't lose focus on your industry and the functional specialty and markets where you can leverage your strengths. Remember that networking is about giving rather than getting, and it's about building relationships with people who feel a level of trust with you.

Networking requires patience and time to build, and it's natural to connect with some people more than others. Leave no stone unturned. You never know who will be able to help you.

Target Marketing Letters

When crafting a target marketing letter, think of the company and executive you're targeting as a client and consider his or her needs. Who is this client and what does he or she need? Who are the client's customers? What does the client need in order to satisfy their customer? What is their customer looking for and how could you help them satisfy their customer better? In order to be able to answer these questions, you need to do research on both the industry and the company; having the knowledge and information will differentiate you as a candidate. Additionally, the research will help prepare you for unexpected calls you may get from the company or the person qualifying candidates.

Next, think about how you can make your case for why *you* are the solution. How will your ideas solve the problem or exploit the possibility? How are your ideas better than other ways to do those things? Why should the client listen to you? Reframe your career as a business story and assemble the resources you need to make your case believable.

The following is an example of how you can build on your statement of value and put it into a story format that is interesting and targets an executive's need.

In your 10K report to investors, one of the outlined initiatives is to increase your gross margins by outsourcing and improving internal efficiencies. At Richmond Technology Partners, I solved similar challenges by developing methodologies that increased their margins from 21% to 39%, on average, by moving marketing efforts and sales to other channels. I developed a program that strategically placed and resold the company's product through 700 value-added resellers, reducing their internal cost of implementing and managing the process. The program was profiled in XYZ's publication, and the positive press, along with the impact on efficiencies and sales, raised margins an additional 9%, or $8.7 million.

What executive wouldn't listen to you or open the door and want to know more about you when approached with a statement that is focused on money, has the potential of a strong value, and is targeted to an executive's objectives or a company's needs?

Even if the company doesn't have a position available, what executive wouldn't want to create a position for a candidate who has a history and background of positive impact? From a competitive standpoint, what executive would want you taking your talents to a competitor?

Without a letter that gets attention, arouses interest, stimulates desire, and has a call for action, you will get a limited response or no response.

Following is an example of a letter to use for "spot opportunities" in companies that are in an acquisition and growth mode or undergoing a change in management.

Dear Mr./Ms.

Today's *Wall Street Journal* indicated that you are acquiring firms that have a solid strategic position in the marketplace, but are struggling and losing money in the current economy. With the industry and companies you're targeting, you may have a need for a strong turnaround executive.

I have twenty years of solid experience in growing and facing the challenges of small to mid-sized companies and larger industry leaders. I have consistently used strategic solutions, have a business development background, and have been a change agent in revitalizing products, launching new products, turning around profitability, and building sales channels to drive revenue and reduce the cost of business.

In my recent position as vice president for XYZ Software in Seattle, I revamped a poorly designed marketing plan, rebuilt the direct-sales force, expanded distribution channels, developed a strategy that reduced internal costs, and launched new products via 7,000 value-added resellers, using Web-based technology. As a result, in the first year, I increased market share by 28% and increased sales by 39%.

In a previous position at Decision Data Inc., I developed the sales force and established the strategy to fund, develop, launch, and market a new service and product offering. In the first year, I put together a $5 million funding package through a third party, developed a strategy to leverage outside development resources to launch the product ahead of schedule, and achieved $2.5 million in new sales. My success in stimulating growth and achieving bottom-line results comes from putting in place assertive, yet practical, action plans that improved efficiencies and reduced the cost of development, marketing, and sales.

I am confident that I have the experience and personal dynamics to move struggling companies to growth and profitability. I would appreciate the opportunity to meet with you to discuss how my background and abilities can meet the needs of your company in driving new growth in your acquisitions and improve your bottom line profitability.

I look forward to speaking with you soon. My résumé is attached.

Sincerely,

Bill Peterson

Sample Letters to CEOs

The following are examples of using different techniques to deliver the same message. The first letter brings attention to a goal set by the board of directors. The second letter is focused on background and value based on experience. Depending on how you choose to approach your target, the following formats can be used as templates to target your prospective contact and company.

Dear Mr./Ms.

Recently, you stated to the board of directors your goal of correcting the downturn in profits, generating new growth, and reducing internal expense. These are the same challenges I faced while achieving a 39% increase in profits and a 12% growth rate yearly for the past three years.

In my recent position as vice president for XYZ Software in Seattle, I revamped a poorly designed marketing plan, rebuilt the direct-sales force, expanded distribution channels, developed a strategy that reduced internal costs, and launched new products via 7,000 value-added resellers, using Web-based technology. As a result, I increased market share by 28% and increased sales by 39% in the first year.

In a previous position at Decision Data Inc., I developed the sales force and established the strategy to fund, develop, launch, and market a new service and product offering. In the first year, I put together a $5 million funding package through a third party, developed a strategy to leverage outside development resources to launch the product ahead of schedule, and achieved $2.5 million in new sales. My success in stimulating growth and achieving bottom-line results comes from putting in place assertive, yet practical, action plans that improved efficiencies and reduced the cost of development, marketing, and sales.

I would like the opportunity to share the strategies I used and to ask if you know of any companies where I can use my expertise to help them capture market share, increase profits, and generate new growth.

I will call you next Friday morning at 9:00 a.m. to coordinate our schedules for an appointment in the near future.

Sincerely,

Bill Peterson

Dear Mr. Potenza:

From my experience with the Center for Entrepreneurial Development, I am aware that you need to search for second-stage management as often as you recruit for start-ups, and that turnaround experience is a part of your criteria. My start-up and turnaround experience are significant.

I have developed executive skills in Fortune 500 software and service companies, and worked directly in developing and providing solutions for companies such as IBM, VISA, MasterCard, First Data Corp., Foodland, and Brunswick Corp. My experience covers growth through such positions as director, division vice president, senior vice president, and president.

Entrepreneurial by nature, and with a strong background in start-ups, turnarounds, business development, and international negotiations, I have more than a decade of experience in starting new divisions, developing outside resources for funding solutions in turnarounds and product development, plus launching new products and processes that generated over $10 million in annual revenue. I have consistently increased sales, expanded market share, reduced costs, and streamlined operations in a wide range of situations.

As a venture capitalist, you are close to and aware of new business opportunities that develop in the software and financial information industry. With that in mind, I would like to schedule a short meeting where we can exchange information and industry knowledge.

I will call you next Tuesday at 9:00 a.m. to schedule a time when we can meet.

Attached is a copy of my résumé.

Thank you in advance for your time.

Sincerely,

Bill Peterson

CHAPTER 9

Creating a Position for Yourself

*"Job security is gone. The driving force of a career
must come from the individual."*
— HOMA BAHRAMI

HIRING THE RIGHT PERSON for the right job is such a difficult task that companies invest thousands of dollars in recruiters, psychometric profiles, screening through résumé services, and HR departments just to get what is needed—a person who is a good fit with the company's chemistry and has the required skills for the job.

What do you think a company would pay to hire a person who has the right skills, knowledge, passion for the job, and desire to succeed? Do you think this individual would drive growth, productivity, be more efficient, work smart, and contribute to the overall company from a profitability standpoint? Do you think a company would create a position for the right person?

Even when facing tough financial challenges and economic downturns, companies will hire talented people they believe will grow and make a difference in their organization. The only ways companies discover or find the talent and create positions are through networking and through people who have identified their fit with the organization, are passionate about what the organization does or represents, have created a strategy, and have implemented a targeted effort and self-marketing plan to get themselves introduced to management.

Targeting Opportunities

You can create job opportunities when no openings exist. The best companies for creating executive positions are those companies that:

- Are growing rapidly
- Are launching new products
- Are forming new divisions
- Are acquiring other companies or reorganizing

Companies that fit the above profiles need good people from other industries and will generally move quickly to create new positions. Well-connected executives with interests in many organizations can provide avenues of opportunity and contacts in companies at senior levels. When there is a compelling reason for hiring, entrepreneurs in small and mid-sized organizations will make internal changes quickly and create positions.

Once you've identified the type(s) of position(s) that match your background, personality and skills (which you identified when you took the suggested assessments outlined in Chapter 2, "Finding the Right Fit"), use the Target Marketing forms in the Appendix to research companies that hire for such positions.

Unmet Needs

Look around your industry for unmet needs and work that requires your set of skills. Find the biggest problem your target company or prospective employer faces, and for which your desires, abilities, temperament, and skills are the solution. Stop thinking like an employee or job applicant and start thinking like an opportunity-minded vendor, scanning the market for work and ferreting out opportunities.

Next, identify a potential employer and target market likely to value your talents and capabilities. Make sure your value proposition is aligned with the company chemistry and initiatives and is easy to understand. Be concise about what you will do and deliver to the targeted organization. Your promise of value must be substantial enough for the executive and the company to make an investment in you. Through your research, find key decision-makers and managers who have hiring capabilities and the ability to create positions in your targeted companies. Once you've identified the key people, begin networking with the goal to establish direct contact, preferably through an introduction you made while networking.

E-mail can be used very effectively and can bypass administrative managers and people who screen executives' calls. After the e-mail, follow up with a phone call. The phone call establishes your credibility and gives you an opportunity to build rapport.

On the Phone

When you get phone time with an executive, you have the opportunity to start building a relationship. As stated earlier, you must deliver value, whether it provides a solution, information, or shares knowledge.

Example:

"Mr. Franklin, I have a specific reason for calling you. I know your line of business and something of the processes you use. During the past 15 months, I have been able to save a company like yours approximately $850,000. I would like to share the details with you. Does your schedule permit a meeting this week?"

The "maybe you or someone you know can help me" approach:

"Hi, Mr. Ellis, I'm Tom Cole. Perhaps you can help me. After reading the recent *Fortune* article, I wondered if you could refer me to, or know of someone who could refer me to . . ."

Use this approach with people who have been promoted to a new position or recently joined an organization.

If you're told that the person you want to contact is out, the best response is, "Thanks. Maybe you can help me. When is a good time to call and reach _____?"

Opening Statements

When using the following statements, put the following phrase at the end of each one—"So what?" That is what the person you are addressing is thinking. You must be prepared to answer the "so what" question with a value proposition that gives you the opportunity to leverage it into an action and the next step.

"Considering what is happening to the technology of your business, I know I can be very useful to you because of my background and experience in _____, where I used my _____ to (increase, grow, improve etc.) _____."

"In your annual report, I read that the company is expanding in the sales area and that Richmond Technology is investing heavily in biopharmaceuticals. While developing new business channels to improve sales 150%, I faced similar challenges to those mentioned in your report, and thought you would benefit by learning some of the methodologies we used for the solutions. Additionally, I noticed we are alums from the UVA. What does your schedule look like for coffee or lunch?"

"My friend (or, a mutual friend, a colleague of mine), _____, suggested that I make a point of contacting you. You may recall from my letter/e-mail, I have experience in building the new division that piloted a product similar to the one you are scheduled to roll out. Given my background, we can collaborate on the challenges with _____ in a way that benefits your bottom line."

"With my background in _____ and the recent news about _____, I thought I should get in touch with you. When is a convenient time one morning that we could have a 15-minute conversation?" (Don't forget to be prepared to answer the question why this person should give you their time. What do you have that is of value and interest to this person, his/her company, goals, or challenges?)

"Mr. _____, your company has a reputation for market-leading products. I'd like to schedule an appointment with you to explain how I could contribute to your company's reputation through my work in _____, where efficiencies were improved 180% and $1.3 million in savings was added to the company's profits. Do you have a half hour free next Tuesday?"

Once you have an interview set up, you'll need to prepare yourself in other ways.

In an Interview

When you finally do get an interview with a decision-maker, do your due diligence. Identify and understand the company's needs and its vision. Make sure your benefit and value proposition are clear and significant. What ideas do you have that will deliver your promise of value? What is it about your experience, background, and successes that make you confident your ideas will work? How well do you understand the target company, its problems, and its opportunities?

When discussing the requirements for a position be sure to distinguish between arbitrary requirements—credentials, degrees, titles, and industry experience—and those that relate to results. Results will be dependent on your skill set and how you handled past challenges.

To set the stage for an exchange of ideas, make sure you use a consultative approach and tone with the executive you're addressing. A strategic and brainstorming-oriented approach is a good way to gain rapport, mutual buy-in, and ownership of the solution. It's also an opportunity for you to understand the areas in the company where you can help or make an impact.

Example:

"I was wondering about your impression of the following, and how you would approach the challenge." (Based on results you have achieved, map out your solution.)

Find out how the executive views the problem.

> What are the key challenges?
> What is his/her "hot button"?
> Where are his/her priorities?
> What attempts have been made in the past?
> How much progress has been made?

By asking key, well-thought-out questions and listening carefully, you will find out what an executive really wants. Then make positive comments in response to his or her remarks. Get her to share her thoughts and vision for the company. Only when the executive starts to consider the positive impact you will have and the favorable impact on the executive's initiatives and goals, will she then consider creating a position. If you're able to accomplish this in your first audience with the senior executive, you'll have the chance for a second interview.

So, how do you generate the level of interest required for an invitation to the next step in the process? Focus your conversations on the future, where the executive pictures the company already benefiting from your contribution and where he or she begins to anticipate specific benefits by relating them directly to your talents. One of the best tools to use for creating interest and enthusiasm is using stories tied to your accomplishments, skills, and abilities.

Create a Lasting Impression Using Stories

Using stories about how you leveraged your specific skills to solve problems will set you apart from other applicants and enable a potential employer or recruiter to relate to you better and remember you.

To ensure that the points you make in your stories are remembered, use the CORE method for creating interesting stories. This means combining a **Circumstance** or situation with an **Opportunity**, and **Resources** used or actions you took that delivered an **End Result** or solution. CORE offers a process for describing your attributes and experiences in a compelling way, combined with information about your history and accomplishments.

The CORE Process

Circumstance: Describe a job by reviewing the circumstance and situation when you began. Make it interesting.

Opportunities: Use information about the opportunities that a job presented. An example would be: "When I joined XYZ company, sales had been falling off for three years, along with a loss or reduction in staff. Understanding the company's markets, I saw the opportunity to target new areas."

Resources: Identify how you used either internal or external resources to create a solution, and the actions taken by you and other members of your team or executive staff. Combining resources and talents with actions is the foundation, the central point, and the most important part of creating your story and developing the CORE process.

End Result: Once you have developed and created the foundation for your story, focus on the quantitative results delivered and/or achieved.

CORE means telling your whole story. Told well, it will generate more genuine interest than any explanation of your past duties. When you talk about your end results, make sure to quantify them. For example, you cut costs by $150,000, or 20%.

In cases where you cannot quantify the results, you need to measure results by using statements tied to efficiencies and financial impact, such as: "I did it in half the time," or "The system I developed was adopted throughout the company."

When you're describing a result or an accomplishment, it is extremely important to indicate the positive things you did to help your organization and how you took on extra tasks. Describe how you helped your management team meet its goals and the results the team achieved. During your depiction of the result, show how you demonstrated a skill, a special knowledge, or a personal quality.

Use the CORE principle to develop stories that cover situations where you can demonstrate the value of creative thinking or problem solving to improve productivity, or to show that you've previously solved a variety of problems.

Employers need to feel that you have the attributes and abilities to give them a solution to one or more of their problems. Your job is to sell them on your ability through your communications and stories that show how you met or exceeded the needs and challenges of past employers in various environments, with the end goal being that you can do the same for them.

The idea is to have several stories that demonstrate the benefits you're bringing to the organization. Don't be shy in describing how you impacted efficiencies and profits, and how, through your efforts, motivated staff in a way that enabled your company to gain market share and/or reduce costs.

Wherever possible, quantify with dollar amounts, percentages, and staff improvements. If you have many stories, focus on the most important. Always keep in mind the position you're seeking and select stories that will best position you for your new role.

When developing your stories, create an outline and practice them on your friends and your spouse. Practice at home and in the car. Use a small recorder or rehearse in front of a mirror. Face your fear and realize you will probably make mistakes until you're comfortable with your story. Attending networking functions is one of the best ways to practice.

Examples of CORE Stories
Circumstance and Opportunity: When I joined XYZ, the company had lost all but four employees and had seen no new revenue for four years. I recognized an opportunity to employ my background in start-ups and my experience in business development and marketing.

Resources: With the help of a third party and an advertising agency, I relaunched the brand and created new advertising and a channel campaign, while spending zero dollars.

End Result: Within 90 days, the first sale was made, and within a year, we had a $4 million gain, representing 60% of the firm's profits.

Circumstance and Opportunity: Our company recruited 200 people a year, but didn't have a good training program in place.

Resources: I created a management-training course. With a staff of 12, we developed a process of logical steps based on our research, and structured a new methodology and course materials.

End result: The company was able to bring in recruits who were a better fit for the company's culture and were able to take on responsibilities within four weeks. The following year, both sales and profits increased more than 28%.

Be Comfortable With Who You Are

When using self-promotion techniques and networking, it's important to be honest with yourself and come to terms with your strengths and vulnerabilities. If you're not honest and comfortable with yourself, you won't project yourself with confidence, and it will be obvious. You have to accept who you are, and not try to be someone you're not, thinking that it will impress those around you. Confidence and being relaxed in your own skin creates a special appeal that will set you apart and differentiate you from the rest of the candidates.

When you're comfortable with yourself, you will find that your focus shifts from one of being self-oriented to one of helping others. You will always create a positive impact if you can direct clients and others around you, to someone else as a way of providing a solution and perhaps shortening their time and effort on a project. It shows that you have integrity, honesty, forthrightness, and professionalism, which will set you apart and again, enable you to differentiate yourself. Focusing on others and facilitating solutions is a reciprocal exercise that will not only generate respect, but also, recognition.

Personality plays a role when companies consider you for a position and the fit you will have within their organizations. Automatic Data Processing Inc. (ADP) has gone to extensive lengths to identify personality traits of successful people in various positions. Combining personality traits and a person's knowledge can help to determine how well an individual will fit and how successful they can be within the organization. So, how important is it to position yourself with companies that fit your personality and who you are? More employment decisions are based on personality and chemistry than any other factor. For example, "He's professional and quick-thinking. I like him. Better yet, I trust him. He'll get along with our team and provide the leadership we need. We need to get him onboard."

You've got the contacts through your networking, now you need to sell yourself to a prospective employer. Chapter 10 will give you examples of how to prepare for a successful interview by presenting yourself in a positive, intelligent and forthright manner.

Interviewing

"Experience is not what happens to you; it is what
you do with what happens to you."
— ALDOUS HUXLEY

Prepping for the Interview

You've done everything right and made it through the initial stages of getting your target company's interest and are scheduled for your first round of interviews with the human resources department. In a case where your contact and the person scheduling the interview is a recruiter, he/she has recognized that you have the education and history that match the job requirements.

Most human resource departments schedule the first interview as a telephone interview and will generally ask to schedule a time that is convenient for you. However, some companies and recruiters may want to interview you when you answer the phone. In a situation where you're caught off guard and the interviewer asks if now is a good time, take control of the situation and set an appointment in the immediate future for the phone interview; it will improve your odds for success and you will be better prepared. Don't be afraid that the interviewer won't call you back. If you don't receive a call back, you've just saved yourself a lot of trouble of going through a process that was destined to be unfavorable. You want to work for a company or with a recruiter that respects you and your time. Always remember that the interviewing process is a two-way street. The reason you're being interviewed is because you have the talent and skills that the company is looking to acquire. Align yourself with recruiters and work for companies that fit with your values; otherwise, you may find yourself in an uncomfortable situation, wondering why you ever accepted the position.

When you're setting up your interview, pick a quiet time when you will be undisturbed during the interview process. Never begin a phone interview while you're driving, in a noisy location, or at a location where you cannot speak freely. Take time to practice your interviewing techniques. In telephone interviews, the interviewer is focused on how you come across on the phone, how well you listen, your knowledge of the company, and your enthusiasm. Have your résumé out, along with the information and detail sheets you completed when researching and targeting the company. These forms are located in the Appendix and at *www.overthegap.com*. Make sure you have the challenges the company and its executives are facing and an outline of the stories you will share that show how you used your knowledge, experience and skills to solve problems relative to the company's current challenges. Use a three-ring binder to hold your résumé and the completed forms you downloaded from *www.overthegap.com*. With a three-ring binder, it's easy to flip to sections and access the information you need without stumbling through your answers. It will give you not only the organization you need, but will make you come across to the interviewer as prepared and professional.

Carefully Worded Questions

Have a list of carefully worded questions to ask that will help you gain clarity about the position, the company's and management's goals, and what they want to accomplish. Find out what is the most dominant skill or trait they are looking for and what obstacles are preventing them from reaching their goals. What you want to accomplish with your questioning is not only determining how well you fit with the company, but gaining information that will enable you to articulate in a story format the conversation and statements that establish your skills, background, and experience as the solution that will eliminate their obstacles.

Face-to-Face Interviews

For your initial interview, be sure you arrive at the location 20 minutes ahead of time. Always allow additional time for traffic and getting lost if you don't have a GPS or are not familiar with the area. Use the extra time to review your notes, the forms (from the Appendix of this book) that you filled out, and information you've gathered that is relative to recent positioning statements made by executives in news articles or newly released information on the company Website. If you know the names of the individuals with whom you will be interviewing, have information on statements they may have made, their backgrounds, universities they attended, if they are married, single, or have a family, and awards they may have received. This information will help you with your conversation, and you may find that you have common interests. The goal of having all this information is not only to develop a rapport, but also to provide you with tools to develop a relationship and find common ground. Your due diligence and knowledge of your interviewers' backgrounds will help you determine how well you fit within the company and indicates not only your interest in the company but in becoming part of the organization.

Key Points to Remember

- We all make our initial judgment of people within the first ten to fifteen seconds of meeting them.
- Be confident. Understand that it's natural to be nervous and experience some fear when you're interviewing; so does everyone else.
- Shake hands firmly and maintain direct eye contact. Keep a handkerchief in your pocket and squeeze it to eliminate any chance of having wet or moist palms. If you don't have pockets, be as inconspicuous as possible and grasp the edge of your coat, skirt, or garment to dry your hand.
- Use a breath mint or similar product to keep your breath fresh.
- Maintain a high level of energy.
- Be polite to administrative assistants and try to engage them in small talk. Office personnel are great sources of information.
- Listen carefully to each question you're asked. Ask for clarification if necessary, and make sure you answer each question completely.
- Be prepared to give at least eight examples in which you can demonstrate your ability and action to solve a problem, challenge, or issue that is similar to the challenges facing the company with which you are interviewing. Describe situations that started out negatively and ended with a positive solution, or with you making the best of the not-so-perfect outcome, and examples of how you achieved your goals and the accomplishments you've made. Make sure your examples are varied. If you use a team effort as an example, describe not only the situation but also the specific role you played in the overall team effort.
- Keep your résumé handy and use it as a guide when answering interview questions.

Typical Interview Questions

Answering interview questions is stressful. Most people tend to provide more information than necessary when they are stressed or nervous. When responding to interview questions, give answers that are directly to the point. Be as relaxed as possible. Frame your answers using the CORE method described in Chapter 9. Focus on how you impacted productivity and efficiencies, reduced cost, increased revenue, built teams, solved problems, and met or exceeded the company's goals and challenges.

Use the two-minute drill you developed in Chapter 4 as a foundation for starting the interview. By offering to give the interviewer information on your background, or when you are in the initial stages of the interview, the two-minute drill helps you not only take the pressure off direct questions, but will ease the process for both you and the interviewer. If you don't get the chance to start the interview process and are asked to "Tell me about yourself," use the two-minute drill to set the stage for questions relative to your strengths and the skills you've used to make significant impacts. Additionally, the two-minute drill will help establish the tone for the conversation, making it less formal and allowing you to express yourself, build rapport, and possibly eliminate some of the direct questioning that happens in most interviews.

No matter how experienced you are in interviewing, it's almost impossible to escape some of the direct questioning that HR managers utilize. Most of the questions used by HR staff and interviewers are designed to see if you are consistent in your responses and to identify if your skills, experience, personality, and chemistry will work within the company and the position for which you are applying. Some companies use psychometric tools to evaluate if a candidate will be an asset and a good fit. You may take a psychometric test and be asked a series of questions similar to those that follow and others covered in this chapter. Use this list of typical interview questions to prep for your interview and develop your answers in advance.

What are your greatest weaknesses?

You want to have an answer that takes the focus off your weakness and emphasizes your strengths. Maybe you don't multitask well, in which case you may have created solutions that leveraged the expertise of others, or systems and technologies, to help you manage multiple activities.

| *Weaknesses* | *How you used your skill or knowledge to turn it into a strength* |

1)

2)

3)

What do you do in your spare time?

Interviewers ask this question to find out how balanced you are in managing your work requirements relative to your personal life. Companies avoid workaholics because of traditional problems associated with them. What all companies want, though, is a dedicated staff that will do what it takes to meet the company's challenges. Frame your answer relative to being a team player and doing what it takes, but also how you balance your time away from the office to have fun and fulfill your personal responsibilities. List your hobbies, sports, and things you do to burn off stress, like tennis, golf, or biking.

How can you contribute to this company?

Use the research you did on the company, as well as the answers on your Target Lead Sheet (Form 3 in the Appendix) to showcase how you successfully addressed similar challenges in previous situations with competence and enthusiasm.

Why should I hire you?

The assessments you took and the work you did in Chapters 1 through 4, along with the information you gathered by networking and using other resources, like LinkedIn, will help you utilize a story format that shows your passion for the job, business, or industry.

Why do you want to work for our company?

If you didn't show enough passion or address the "Why should I hire you?" question well enough, they will follow up with the above question. Frame your answer in relation to the information you pulled together when researching the company, and how you fit from a personality, knowledge, skill, and solution-oriented style relative to the company and position.

What interests you most about this job and position?

Base your answer on the information you gathered while answering the questions for filling out the forms as well as the assessments you took that helped you identify the types of industries and jobs in which you will be successful. Use the CORE process to explain how much you enjoy the challenges and opportunities this type of position presents to you in relation to your skills and experience.

Where do you hope to be in five years?

All companies are looking for stability in the people they hire and want candidates that will contribute to the growth and success of the company. A company makes a substantial investment when they hire you. The internal cost alone is between 30% and 37% above your salary to bring you onboard, not to mention additional training or products needed for you to perform your job. Given all of the hard and soft costs to bring a person onboard, it could cost a company as much as two or three times your salary the first year. From a purely business standpoint, the company will want to recoup its investment and gain a return for hiring you.

During the conversation, be absolutely certain to provide examples of how you will be an asset and that the investment the company is making in you is not the only investment being made; that you, too, will be investing in the company and are passionate about being able to drive the growth the company needs to succeed.

Note: Because the cost is so high to bring executives and managers onboard, the current trend in many companies is to hire executives on a contract basis to reduce their internal costs. Interestingly, the generation filling the gap created by exiting boomers expects to have as many as 20 or more jobs in their careers. Ultimately, we are all the CEO of our own company, Me Inc., and responsible for our successes, either as our own company or when investing our time and effort in solving the problems and challenges facing other companies.

What are your career goals?

What are your short- and long-term goals? When you look into the future, what new skills do you want to learn, what certifications do you want to have that will increase your value to a company, and what goals do you want to achieve?

List short-term goals relative to two- and three-year goals and your long-term goals as five-year goals.

Tell me about some of your greatest accomplishments.
Use stories that expound on past accomplishments, a problem you solved, or a goal you reached; stories that are related to the challenges the company is facing and the job requirements.

Why are you looking for another job?
Be positive in your comments. Do not say anything negative about your current employer or, if you were displaced, a past employer. Address your answers honestly and relative to growth, challenges, and desires in relation to your future goals and the contributions you want to make.

Are you applying for other jobs?
Make sure your answer indicates that any other positions and jobs you are applying for are similar positions.

What do you like most about your current job? What do you like least about your current job?
Your answers to these questions will be used to determine how well you will fit in a company or organization and gives clues to the type of environment in which you want to work, whether as part of a team or as an opportunity to learn where you will be able to be creative or manage multiple challenges. Orient your responses to what you have found out about the company and the position. In responding to what you like least, use examples that you are unlikely to find in the company and position for which you are applying. Do not say anything negative about your current or past employer. Create a list of what you enjoy most in your current position, what you like least, and your response to each item on the list.

How do you feel about working for a manager who is younger than you?
This type of question generally means that you will be reporting to a person who is younger than you, and you may be asked if you like working with a manager who is of the opposite sex. Respond in a manner that is focused on the individual's capability, what you can learn from him/her, and how that knowledge will improve your potential to meet the company's challenges.

What is the most difficult situation you have had to face?

Orient your response in relation to a problem and solution using the CORE system. You want to take this opportunity to show how well you handled challenges that were out of your comfort zone and had a strong impact on your organization, team, or company.

What is your current compensation package and salary?

Include your salary, bonuses, commissions, benefits, perks, and vacation package. If you are scheduled to get an increase in salary, provide the percentage along with any other increases or incentives you are expecting.

What type of compensation or what income range do you require?

A safe statement would be that you're looking for the right opportunity and that if you are the best candidate for the position, you're confident that you will be offered compensation that is standard for the industry and your level of experience. In situations where you know the company cannot meet your initial requirements, you may be able to negotiate other terms to meet your needs. If you are passionate about the company and the opportunities and challenges it presents, make an effort to work with the company; you will come across as authentic and sincere in your desire to be a strong contributor and team player.

How willing are you to relocate?

Even though technology is making it possible to work from almost anywhere, companies will move executives and key people who drive change, growth, and results. If you are not willing to relocate at the present, don't close the door on the opportunity; state that while at the present it isn't feasible for you, relocating in the future may be a possibility.

If relocation is required, make sure that the company will provide you a tour of the area so you can determine if it is a location that meets your needs and requirements. In the event that the company is acquired or falls on hard times, make sure you are going to be satisfied with where you would be relocated, that the area provides opportunity for you and your family, and that you will be comfortable with the location for the next five to ten years.

What causes you to lose your temper?

Everyone loses his/her temper. Don't say that you haven't lost your temper at work; you won't be believed. Use examples, such as backstabbing, people who are habitually late to meetings, and blame shifting, as suitable answers.

What is your leadership style?

A good leader will use a mix of the four basic leadership styles: dictatorial, authoritative, consultative and participative. Your best response would be to show how you have used a participative style when working with creative people, a consultative leadership approach with people who have skill and experience, a more dictatorial style for those who lack full motivation and are arrogant. Authoritative style is used when there is a lack of direction; it provides vision and gives staff the autonomy to develop solutions in relation to their goals.

What was your most challenging experience in dealing with a coworker?

Select an example where you were able to turn a situation around from a negative into a positive, one that impacted the company positively or resolved a conflict that was preventing production or efficiencies, and the process you used to make it happen.

Behavioral-Based Interviews

If you are unfamiliar with behavioral-based interviews, or challenged by them, you may want to consider hiring a career coach who is experienced in behavioral interviewing to help you prepare and be more successful in answering the questions.

The purpose of behavioral interviews is to determine your qualification and fit or "placeability."

Behavioral-based interviews are designed to be conversational, where both parties, through the exchange of information, allow themselves to mutually arrive at a commitment and decision. When responding to behavior-based interview questions, use the CORE approach outlined in Chapter 9.

The four types of questions usually used during a behavioral-based interview are:

1. Fact-finding questions that verify stated information on your résumé.
2. Technical questions to assess your expertise.

3. Behavioral questions that will evaluate your potential effectiveness in the new position by asking you to share past experiences that are relevant to the company's goals and the current opportunity.
4. Hypothetical questions are used to predict how you will perform in a future situation. These types of questions will start with the interviewer asking you to imagine yourself in a situation, or begin with "What if" questions.

Interviewers trained in behavioral interviewing will listen for the use of *I* and *we* statements to determine team orientation, consistency, and confidence, as well as the tone, inflection, and delivery of your replies to ensure that you're fully answering the question or if you're deflecting, and to see if you're putting a positive spin on everything.

Below are examples of typical behavioral-based interview questions.

> Describe a situation where you were able to use persuasion to convince someone to see things your way.

> Describe a time you used your coping skills when you were faced with a stressful situation.

> Give me an example of when you used good judgment and logic to solve a problem.

> Give me an example of when you established a goal and were able to achieve or exceed it.

> Tell me about a time when you used your presentation skills to influence a person's opinion.

> Tell me about a situation in which your persistence paid off.

> Describe a time you failed to reach a goal and how it affected you.

> Describe a situation when you had to gain an appreciation and understanding of someone else's viewpoint before you

could complete your job. What challenges did this create and how did you handle them?

Tell me about a situation when you had a personal commitment that conflicted with an emergency business meeting. What did you do?

When faced with having to make an unpopular decision or announcement, tell me how you handled it.

Tell me about a difficult decision you had to make this year.

Give me an example of a time you motivated others.

Give me an example of how you used your fact-finding skills to solve a problem.

Give me an example of a time when you delegated a project effectively.

Tell me about a time when you had to make a split-second decision.

Asking the Right Questions

If you didn't get a chance to explore what the company's dominant skills or requirements are when you were answering the interviewer's questions, by following up with intelligent questions you will impress the interviewer and indicate that you have a grasp of the company's challenges and understand what is expected to be a match for the position. The right questions will express your need to be challenged and excited by the opportunities the position provides.

Consider using some of the following questions.

What is the greatest challenge that this position will have?

Is this a new or existing position?

Was the person in this position promoted or did they leave the company?

What has been the turnover or rate of attrition in this position?

What is the leadership style of the person to whom I will be reporting?

How would you describe a typical day for someone in this position?

How would you describe the financial outlook of the company?

What are the company's growth projections?

What are the goals and objectives of the company?

What are the goals and objectives of this position?

How will you know you have hired the right person?

How well do you think I would fit in the company and in this position?

Has there been downsizing in the company?

Describe how downsizing requirements are handled and processed.

Do you have any concerns about my skills or me?

When you're satisfied that you have asked all the questions you need to determine if the position is one that is a good fit for you, and one that will challenge you and enable you to grow professionally and personally, end the interview by asking for the job.

When you ask for the job, reiterate how your skills, expertise and knowledge will not only meet the needs and requirements of the company, but contribute to its growth. Finally, state that you like what you've heard, and ask about the next step.

The Next Step

With a successful interview now behind you and an offer from the HR manager, be sure you're also comfortable with the fit, challenge and opportunity that this position and company have to offer. Next you'll need to:

1. Define and accept the compensation package based on industry standards for the position, title, and requirements.
2. Accept the offer, pending receipt of a written offer from the company.
3. Determine how, and if, you will handle a counteroffer from your current employer.

After the Interview

I strongly recommend that you follow up within 24 hours of your interview. You will want to make contact via e-mail, and via a thank-you note mailed the day following your interview, at the latest. Use monarch-sized notepaper for your thank-you note, if possible. Make sure your thank-you note is handwritten and that your business card is included. Using your branded-value proposition and CORE examples in your thank-you note, bullet the challenges the company and executive faces relative to the skills, expertise, and background you have that will solve their problem. Some people have typed the bulleted points and their CORE responses with a short handwritten thank-you note at the bottom of the page.

If you need examples of what a thank-you letter should look like, use Google, Bing, Monster, or Career Builder to find a template you want to use and modify to your specific needs.

Counteroffers

Counteroffers are common and a knee-jerk reaction of a company faced with losing a valued employee. If you receive a counteroffer, it is considered unprofessional and even unethical to withdraw your acceptance of the new position because you accepted a counteroffer from your current employer.

Keep in mind that accepting a counteroffer from your current employer presents the risk that the time you remain will be used to find a replacement and you'll be fired at a later date.

Accepting counteroffers is high-risk. If you do accept a counteroffer, make sure the incentive you receive is large enough to financially support you for more than a two-year time period. Why?

Accepting a counteroffer puts your loyalty in question. When it comes time for raises and incentives, your lack of loyalty will be remembered.

Which employees will be the first to go when it's time for cutbacks and downsizing?

And, circumstances that caused you to consider a change will more than likely repeat themselves in the future.

EPILOGUE

The Benefit of Personal Coaching

"To succeed requires all the dedication and effort that you can muster because your success will ultimately relate to an ongoing and persistent effort. It's a marathon and not a sprint to the finish line."
— DAVID PATTERSON

NCLUDED IN THE COST OF THIS BOOK is a free initial consultation as well as a 60% discount on a career coaching session with an experienced certified coach. The coach will work with you during the initial consultation and subsequent session to jumpstart your job search and career transition process. As you work through the exercises in this book, consider when and how you'll want to utilize the services of a coach to establish a game plan for success. In addition to the consultation and career coaching, an assessment valued at $200 is provided to help you reach your goals.

What is a Career Coach?
"What I've found from my experiences is that career coaches provide insight into the workplace, as many come from backgrounds in HR or top-level management where they've done it, seen it, been there. Working with career coaches, you can cover any topic, not just how to get a job. For example: they're well-versed in advice about growing your existing career or position, input on career and job issues, discussing starting your own business, interviewing, and more. I've found career coaches are able to provide tangible advice in areas of career management, too."
— Karina Diaz Kano (Wall Street Journal)

Career coaches provide support to guide you in establishing goals and strategies for a job search campaign. Coaches help ramp up career efforts by working with you to define objectives, develop action plans, and implement and manage the overall process of your campaign. Coaching, in conjunction with the process in this book, is designed to focus on:

- Developing an understanding of your skills, attributes and career fit
- Self-branding
- Target marketing
- Networking campaigns
- Targeted mailings
- Strategies for landing a job or transitioning into a new career

To register for your session with an executive coach, go to *www.overthegap.com*. While you're there, view the biographies of coaches who are participating in this program.

You'll never plough a field by turning it over in your mind.
— IRISH PROVERB

APPENDIX

1. Job Matrix
2. Target Marketing Strategies
3. Target Lead Sheet
4. Research Worksheet
5. SWOT
6. Networking Fact Sheet
7. Networking Contact Profile
8. Daily Success Journal
9. Monthly Success Journal
10. Victory Log

Appendix

*"I don't care how much power, brilliance or energy you have, if you
don't harness it and focus it on a specific target and hold it there, you're
never going to accomplish as much as your ability warrants."*
— ZIG ZIGLAR

THE GREATEST FACTOR IN SUCCESS is the ability to balance the
time invested in your career search, health, family, and recreation. Managing your time through balance enables one to maintain an
organized and systematic effort. In addition to helping stay organized,
balancing keeps you upbeat and provides a good mental attitude.

Maintaining your focus is not necessarily easy. Finding the right job
and career takes time, as does the process to establish the foundation and
efforts needed to land a new job. Like any other business, starting out
with a plan, or blueprint for success will ensure that you make it. Put the
plan in place, follow the process, and be persistent in your efforts until
you succeed.

The forms in this Appendix, along with the exercises in the book,
are designed to work together to build a foundation and help you stay on
task. Ultimately, the level of success achieved is completely up to you and
the effort invested in the process. If you have a strong network in place,
finding employment will not take as long as it will for someone who has
to build one.

To help stay focused and balanced, the forms in the Appendix
enables one to establish goals and record daily and weekly successes,
while keeping a log of monthly achievements. These forms are also

available for downloading from *www.overthegap.com,* after which they may be manipulated to fit your specific needs.

Form # 1—Job Matrix

In order to keep you motivated, this form lists weekly efforts and tracks successes. This form can also be used to identify areas where your goals are not being met. Remember, set goals that stretch your boundaries and make you try new experiences. Be careful not to make the goals unattainable; this will only cause frustration and will have a negative impact on your efforts. Use this form as a tool to maximize your efforts.

If you're not hitting the goals, it may be that they are unrealistic or an indication that you have not researched your target market well enough. An example of an unrealistic goal is: that you will attend three networking events per week and you only have time to attend one. Attending an event where you won't meet the people in your target market is an example of unsuccessful research. These above two examples indicate a waste of time and effort. A more constructive use of your time is to attend one event per week where you'll make contact with people who are knowledgeable and have connections to your target market. This scenario represents a successful use of time and efforts and meets the weekly goal of attending a meeting with like-minded individuals.

How do you find out if an event fits your goal? Clues to watch for are that the event sponsors are on your list of target companies, are in the target market you identified, or the information at the event is tailored, either directly or indirectly, to specific targets.

At the top of the form, enter in the days of the week in the month you will begin your efforts. Note that there is a targeted number representing what each goal is for that specific week. An example would be to target two networking events each week. The actual number of events attended may have been only one. Enter one as the number of events and 50% as the success factor. Make sure that the goals and activities are oriented and aligned with your targets and target market; otherwise, you are wasting time and effort.

Job Matrix

Week of															
Measures	Target	to Actual	%	Target	to Actual	%	Target	to Actual	%	Target	to Actual	%
Events												
Informational calls												
Calls to set up meetings												
New contacts identified												
Meetings held												
Company profiles completed												
Classes/Seminars												
Books read/summarized												
Résumés sent												
Telephone interviews												
On-site interviews												
Online applications												
Thank-you notes and letters												
Follow-up calls												
Exercise												
Just Fun												
Family activity												
Spiritual activity												

Form # 2—Target Marketing Strategies

This template has been filled in with an example showing how to structure a strategy for target marketing. The template is broken down into the following areas:

Definition: Use key phrases and words that identify and define the type of position relative to your target market and the career options that fit your personality, skills, and experience. Then use these key phrases and words to formulate how you're able to impact growth, profitability, efficiencies, and key objectives of the company and executive management.

Invest time thinking about the future. Use this section to summarize where you want to be in both three and five years. Take responsibility for the future and begin building a plan that supports your vision, core capabilities, and branded-value proposition, with an offer that drives a benefit directly related to your target market and companies.

Who is my prospect: Take the information you put together when identifying your target market and the companies you want to target and take it a step further. Write down the types of companies that would be prospects. The criteria used in identifying prospects is those companies that fit your value proposition, skill sets, and those that fit your history of having impacted areas such as cost, stronger customer relationships, or a loss in business: companies whose profiles are a solid match with your personality, skills, background, and expertise.

Forums and media: How can you gain exposure and interact with potential prospects?

Where can you find information on senior executives, the movers and shakers, and the individuals who are visible within the company and market? Drill down into the details on the companies and target market, and then go to the company Websites. Learn everything you can about your customer or targeted company. What magazines would the prospect read? What blogs do they link to? How does the customer interact within the community? How can the prospect find you and become aware of who you are? List all of the media you can or would use to interact with them. Don't neglect activities such as volunteer groups, political organizations, colleges, universities, fraternal organizations, churches, and so on.

Project: In this section, list all the target companies, industries, forums, and media that resulted from your efforts in identifying targets and how you will reach out to them to gain greater visibility. (In addition to just being a listing of actionable items and strategies, the project section can be used to tie actionable items to the Job Matrix.)

Action: Consider and list what actions to take in relation to the project you've identified.

Detail: Refine and define your action. Be specific as to what makes up the action.

By when: Make the actionable items date-specific.

TARGET MARKETING STRATEGIES

Definition	Definition
I am looking for a _____ position where I can use my background in _____ to improve _____ by increasing revenue in _____ and _____, building competitive value, and reducing the overall cost of business. I help *Small to Mid-Sized Businesses* improve *efficiencies* and *process management,* increase *revenue* in *sales* and *marketing,* build competitive value, and reduce the overall cost of business. Long-Term (5 to 8 years) Have a job that provides the opportunity and resources to establish a network to use as leverage in building a consulting company with revenue potential for 10 years and an average annual income over $150k per year.	• Live in DC and travel no more than 30% to 50% of the time. • Starting income minimum of $85k to $125k with an upside of $180 to 200k per year. • The company is a software development or technology company. • The company is forward thinking and nurtures a creative and entrepreneurial spirit. • The company is financially sound, rewards out-of-the-box thinking and is aggressive in its desire to capture market share. • Position enables me to work from home or in a location near a regional airport.

Who is my prospect/customer and how will I find them?	Who is my prospect continued
(Chamber of Commerce list of top Tate County businesses, Washington Post, CED, Top 50 list, Biz Journal, industry magazines and Internet info) • Software companies ○ ERP, BI, BPM, SCM, BPI • New companies • Nonprofit organizations • Energy companies • Small manufacturing • Supply chain/distribution • Customer-centric (lawyers, staffing, CPA) • Companies from 50 to 200 people • Companies doing business in the Southeast • Local RTP company	**Companies that:** • Want to improve efficiencies and business processes • Are suffering from a loss of business • Want to contain costs • Are new or rebranding/launching new products and services • Use ERP applications • Want to develop more efficient ways to grow and thrive in business • Utilize existing customer base and build better customer relationships • Need sales people

What forums or media will I use to interact with potential prospects/customers?
 	
Where would my customers go and what would they read? What is or would be of interest to them? How would they interact within the community? How would my customers find me?
 	
• Career boards/Internet job posting sites
• Networking meetings
   ○ Chamber of Commerce meetings
   ○ Networking meet-up groups
   ○ Execunet sponsored meetings (local)
   ○ Toastmasters
	What forums or media continued
	
	• Local Involvement
	   ○ Volunteer groups (Jimmy Vee, special Olympics—high profile groups)
	   ○ Tennis organizations (act as organizer captain)
	   ○ Political support groups in local government
	   ○ Religious groups/churches
	• Magazine articles
	• Via the Web/blogs

PROJECT	ACTION	DETAIL	BY WHEN/ NEXT STEPS
State Govt.	Review Website and look for opportunities	Reviewed, no opportunities at present Review again in 1 week	Weekly
	ID local groups to get involved in that will provide networking and other opportunities	Chamber of Commerce Transportation meeting	Sept. 11 @ Chamber RSVP by Sept 8th
USA Gov.	Posted résumé Biweekly search	Complete detail on résumé	
20 State companies	Review top 500 and Top 100 NC companies Select companies that fit	Use Chamber of Commerce Fortune 500 list Find out about companies that just moved into the area **ERP/BPI/ BPM/ BI/SCM**	Contact Chamber
IBM	Posted résumé on job site, set up search engine, targeted jobs, sent résumés	Résumés sent to 5 job opportunities	Review Mon., Wed., Fri
SAS	Posted for 2 jobs	Check weekly	Mon., Wed., Fri.
EMC	Checked, no opportunities as yet		
Lab Corp			
Sun Trust			
Global	Sent résumé		
John Deere	Joe 469-3955		

PROJECT	ACTION	DETAIL	BY WHEN/ NEXT STEPS
20 US companies	Review Fortune 5000 companies and break out by industry, growth, IPO early stage funding		
Evapt.com			
SunGuard			
JackBe			
TIBCO			
Pegasystems			
Appian			
Oracle			
SAP			
ModusLink			
Infor			
Optio			
Clarity			
Choice Point			
Blue Vector			
Kintera			
Maugistics			
Sterling Commerce			
SSA GlobalLogility			
Descartes			
Viewlocity			

PROJECT	ACTION	DETAIL	BY WHEN/ NEXT STEPS
RECRUITERS	Review and target industry-specific recruiters by local and national geo.	Target 8 to 10 per week	
Red Book Recruiters by SIC	Pick out specific recruiters Research Websites for fit Call in to recruiter Send résumé	Go through Directory of Executive Recruiters ID recruiters on Tues./Thurs.	
Net Share Job Listings	Review 2 times per week	Go through lists and target specific opportunities—send résumé	Tues., Thurs.
Execunet Listings	Review 2 times per week	Go through lists and target specific opportunities—send résumé	Tues., Thurs.
Monster			
Career Builder			
Nonprofit companies	Target 5 to 10 companies and find out about involvement opportunities and employment	Get a directory or listing of nonprofits in local geo. and in NC.	
Temporary Employment companies			
Manpower			
VC Groups or Companies			

PROJECT	ACTION	DETAIL	BY WHEN / NEXT STEPS
NETWORKING **2 Events per month**			
Chamber of Commerce	ID key local business people you want to meet	See if anyone in network knows contacts. Schedule an appointment for intro/and interview key people	
	ID an event to be involved in	8/26 Business Showcase @ RBC 9/9 After hours @ CEI 9/10 Professional Speaking $25 RSVP 9/04 9/16 120th meeting cost $85 RSVP by 9/2 9/23 Sports Council 1/4ly $25 RSVP 9/16 9/25 Education Forum $15 RSVP 9/19	Biz Showcase 10/26 After Hours 11/9 Professional Speaking 12/10 Sports Council 12/16 Education Forum 10/25
		Senior Employment Fair Bridge Water Field House 499 Deacon Boulevard Winston-Salem, NC	9/08 from 10–2:00
Toastmasters	Leverage membership		
Volunteer Groups	American Cancer Assoc., Am. Heart Assoc., Wake Co./ Gov. Habitat for Humanity	Call Am. Cancer Soc. and get listed as a volunteer	
	Make A Wish Foundation		
Tennis/Health Club Exercise Plan	Set up home exercise plan What is my health worth?	Set up work-out area	8/23
Alumni Assoc.	ID benefits and opportunities	Call and get more information than what is on website	

PROJECT	ACTION	DETAIL	BY WHEN/ NEXT STEPS
On-Line Associations	Sales/Mktg. Assoc.	ID associations using the JJ Hill DB to determine best value for $$	
Business Leadership Mtgs	Briar Creek breakfasts, etc.	ID beginning of Jan. one meeting to get involved in	
CED	Online opportunities/review	Review bimonthly, determine opportunity (primarily pharma, may be opportunity in start-up or for consulting)	
Campbell College	See about the alumni association	Review Website and call	
Sigma Chi national and local	See about alumni benefits for networking, etc.	Go to Website—local and national contact	
MARKETING			
Write Articles	Must be target company oriented. Generalist is considered most valuable in business Articles: Growing market presence Global markets, Increasing Revenue, Cost containment/ efficiencies, Business process re-engineering		
Press Releases			
Web Page/Blog	Revamp site for new layout and load in links		8/25
Book Review	ID one book per month to review that is industry-oriented and brand-oriented		
Speaking Engagements	Find out how to get listed for speaking engagements, etc.		

Form # 3—Target Lead Sheet

The Target Lead Sheet is designed for action and information. Steps are outlined so you can pull together the contact information needed to target prospects and the information available stating the company's challenges. Fill in as much of the information as possible and you will be able to drill down to the key issues and needs of a company and its executives. Once you have identified the initiatives and challenges of the executive staff and the company, use this information, combined with the Research Worksheet, to create a strategy, campaign and communications based on your skills and background that solves or can solve the company's challenges. In addition to being an information resource, you can use this form to review before attending events that your target companies may attend, for phone interviews and in developing opening statements.

Target Lead Sheet

Company Name		
Address		
Phone		
Visited Website		
Company statement by sr. XO		
10K		
CEO		
Pres		
EVP		
Articles/Positioning Statement		
Clip Art (articles of interest based on corporate objectives or competitive information to increase opportunities or solve problems)		
Network Inquiry (solicit network for information about company issues/needs)		
Craft Letter of Introduction and or Cover Letter		
Send Letter of Intro. (appt. can be to interview person about co. for an e-book, etc.)		
Contact internal person (follow-up call to letter and set an appointment)		
Initial Appointment Set		
Thank you letter sent (outline next steps)		
Follow-Up Date/Action Items		

Form # 4—Research Worksheet

Research will be the key to your success when targeting either a company or its executives. The Research Worksheet guides you through a series of steps and questions to help with research and provides the information and knowledge you need to clearly understand the company, the position, and details about key executives. The more you know about statements that key executives and persons of interest have made and that are posted on the company Website or in documents like a 10K, the greater your success will be in landing a job or leveraging the contacts you make to find other opportunities.

RESEARCH WORKSHEET

Company	
Address	

Type of Business	Year Business Started

Financial Status
Number of Employees
Product and Services Description

Name of Contact Person	
Date Contacted	Date to Follow up

Research on Contact Person

Previous company

Known successes, books written, speeches, articles

Articles or public information on this company that indicate growth or loss of business and/or internal changes and hiring practices.

What background and training requirements does this company require?

Who would you be competing with for a position or opening in this field?

How many employees has this company hired in the last year?

What challenges face this company to ensure its growth and competitiveness?

What has prevented this company from exceeding its goals and projections?

What factors have contributed to this company's success?

Personal Observations

Form # 5—SWOT

SWOT is an acronym for strengths, weaknesses, opportunities, and threats that is typically used by sales people in identifying potential sales opportunities. This form works great when tailored to understanding where your strengths fit relative to your target or job, what your targets' weaknesses are relative to your strengths, and where the opportunities are where you can use a CORE story or your two-minute drill to solve or meet a need. The completed SWOT exercise, when combined with the information you put together with the Target Lead Sheet and Research Worksheet, will help you develop the framework for the statements to use in your communications and in orienting your résumé to meet a company's needs or position requirements. This exercise is also great for interview preparation.

SWOT

Strengths (List your strengths in relation to this position and opportunity.)

Weaknesses (List the client's weaknesses and/or needs relative to your strengths.)

Opportunities (Which story or action can you share that will address how you've solved this type of need or challenge in the past?)

Threats (List any weak areas or liabilities and your plan to offset them.)

Form # 6—Networking Fact Sheet

Picture in your mind the end result or goal you want to achieve when attending a networking event. Be clear what types of questions you'll want to ask and prepare accordingly. The Networking Fact Sheet outlines several informative questions and the type of information you want to walk away with after you've connected with someone at a networking event. Being able to provide responses to the types of questions on this sheet enables you to be a valuable resource for your connections and also allows you to clearly articulate the value your connection has to offer. Providing information that clearly identifies a solution for someone you meet at a networking event creates credibility and will differentiate you from other professionals.

NETWORKING FACT SHEET

Date	
Network Contact's Name:	
Company/Organization Name	
How would you describe your best prospect or client?	
What key products or services do you provide or specialize in?	
Where or in what industry, demographic, or market would I find your best prospect or client?	
What values or key attributes do you or your company provide that differentiates you from your competitors?	
Describe or provide an example of how your products or services delivered a solution that impacted your client's efficiencies, profitability, or market share, or one that met or exceeded client expectations.	
How would you recommend I approach a potential prospect? What information would you like for me to hand out or offer?	

Form # 7—Networking Contact Profile

When attending networking events, take several of these forms with you to complete immediately following the event. The Networking Contact Profile Form helps you organize the networking connections you meet. As you begin to network more, you will find that keeping a record of contacts is extremely valuable and can be used for years. Remember the story of Cary in the networking section of the book? Had Cary maintained his connection with his former professor it would, no doubt, have impacted his opportunity for the job he wanted.

Networking Contact Profile

Use this form to list the contacts you've been given from people with whom you network.

Contact Names Received	
Name	Name
Title	Title
Company	Company
Discussion/Description/Challenges (where you or others in your network can add value) Permission to use network contact as point of reference? Best time to contact	Discussion/Description/Challenges (where you or others in your network can add value) Permission to use network contact as point of reference? Best time to contact
E-mail	E-mail
Phone	Phone
Fax	Fax

Form # 8—Daily Success Journal

Use the Daily Success Journal to track your daily successes, both planned and unplanned. For instance, "Washed the dog," "Took the kids for an ice cream cone." Understand that this book is about securing a job, but it is also about balancing your life. No matter what the event is, tracking daily successes helps you stay motivated. Landing a job isn't easy—there are days when you'll feel as though you've made zero progress; this is when you need to refer to the Daily Success Journal. The journal will help you develop a healthier view of your life and efforts. It can even trigger thoughts linked to the next actions that will help you focus and keep you on task and on target.

Make sure you fill out the "Reason Why" section, as this step helps you with focus and thinking of other actions to create future successes. The whole purpose of this section is to stimulate your thought patterns into positive actions that will improve your results and balance.

Filling out the Daily Success Journal, when used in conjunction with the Monthly Success Journal, helps you define you best days, prep days, and relaxation days so you have a clearer understanding of where you have been putting forth your efforts.

DAILY SUCCESS JOURNAL

Day _____   Date_____

SUCCESS	REASON WHY	NEXT ACTION
		Start By _____ Complete By _____
		Start By _____ Complete By _____
		Start By _____ Complete By _____
		Start By _____ Complete By _____

Form # 9—Monthly Success Journal

Use the Monthly Success Journal to track best days, the days you rest or have allocated for other activities, and preparation days for activities oriented toward goals and weekly successes. This form is designed to push you outside of your comfort zone and keep you on a path of improvement.

The "Ultimate Goal" section is for a goal that is just outside your reach, and is designed to push you to go further than you believe you can. Many athletes and successful business people use strategies that challenge and push them beyond their comfort zone. The challenge you select should be one that is just beyond your reach that requires extra effort to accomplish.

The day boxes are for short notes to keep track of activities that day so you can track the number of days that were best, rest, and prep days. Keeping this log helps with the reality of the effort you're making each month relative to successes and goals.

At the bottom of the form are boxes to list books and information that will keep you informed and on your "A game" as well as a list of challenges, incompletes, and problems or issues to address. This section is designed to track the challenges and how well you completed them. Additionally, there are boxes to help identify resources that will help you reach your ultimate goals.

The objective of these forms is to help in maintaining a balance in your life. As important as a job is to your success and survival, you will find that you are more productive in your efforts and more successful when you maintain a healthy balance.

Monthly Success Journal for:

This Month's Ultimate Goal

(A goal that will stretch your boundaries and is slightly beyond your reach)

_____

_____

_____

SUNDAY	MONDAY	TUESDAY	WEDNESDAY
Best | Rest | Prep	Best | Rest | Prep	Best | Rest | Prep	Best | Rest | Prep
Best | Rest | Prep	Best | Rest | Prep	Best | Rest | Prep	Best | Rest | Prep
Best | Rest | Prep	Best | Rest | Prep	Best | Rest | Prep	Best | Rest | Prep
Best | Rest | Prep	Best | Rest | Prep	Best | Rest | Prep	Best | Rest | Prep
Best | Rest | Prep	Best | Rest | Prep	Best | Rest | Prep	Best | Rest | Prep

BOOKS TO READ

1. _____

2. _____

3. _____

CHALLENGES/INCOMPLETES/MESSES TO ADDRESS

1. _____

2. _____

3. _____

TELE-SEMINARS AND MOTIVATIONAL PROGRAMS

_____

_____

_____

WHAT ISN'T WORKING *(be aware of where you are hesitating and plan future tasks based on observations)*

_____

_____

_____

Monthly Success Journal for:

	THURSDAY				FRIDAY				SATURDAY			ACTION ITEMS
	Best	Rest	Prep		Best	Rest	Prep		Best	Rest	Prep	_____
												_____
	Best	Rest	Prep		Best	Rest	Prep		Best	Rest	Prep	_____
												_____
	Best	Rest	Prep		Best	Rest	Prep		Best	Rest	Prep	_____
												_____
	Best	Rest	Prep		Best	Rest	Prep		Best	Rest	Prep	_____
												_____
	Best	Rest	Prep		Best	Rest	Prep		Best	Rest	Prep	_____

WHO DO I NEED TO ASK TO HELP ME REACH MY GOALS?

_____
_____
_____
_____
_____

FOR WHAT?

_____
_____
_____
_____
_____

Form # 10—Victory Log

The Victory Log is for documenting the victories that take you closer to your goals. A victory may be health oriented, such as losing ten pounds or finally going to the gym. It could also be supporting your children by getting involved in sporting activities with them, completing a family budget, refinancing the house, or using LinkedIn to connect with a CEO.

The Victory Log is for big victories, meeting a major challenge, or exceeding expectations. Maybe you made fifteen more contacts this month than you had in your plan or were able to save additional money. You should have at least one major victory a month that brings you closer to your goals.

Victory Log

Log the victories you have accomplished that take you out of your comfort zone and closer to your goals.

_____

_____

_____

_____

_____

_____

_____

_____

_____

_____

_____

_____

_____

_____

Breinigsville, PA USA
16 September 2009
224149BV00003B/1/P